FOOTBALL 🏈 SUPERSTARS

Dan Marino

FOOTBALL ● SUPERSTARS

Tiki Barber

Tom Brady

John Elway

Brett Favre

Peyton Manning

Dan Marino

Donovan McNabb

Joe Montana

Walter Payton

Jerry Rice

Ben Roethlisberger

Barry Sanders

FOOTBALL ● SUPERSTARS

Dan Marino

Jon Sterngass

Checkmark Books™
An imprint of Facts On File, Inc.

DAN MARINO

Checkmark Books
An imprint of Infobase Publishing
132 West 31st Street
New York, NY 10001

Library of Congress Cataloging-in-Publication Data
Sterngass, Jon.
 Dan Marino / Jon Sterngass.
   p. cm. — (Football superstars)
 Includes bibliographical references and index.
 ISBN 978-0-7910-9606-2 (hardcover)
 ISBN 978-1-60413-323-3 (paperback)
 1. Marino, Dan, 1961– 2. Football players—United States—Biography—Juvenile literature.
 3. Quarterbacks (Football)—United States—Biography—Juvenile literature. I. Title. II. Series.

 GV939.M29S83 2008
 796.332092—dc22
 [B]
                 2007040950

Checkmark Books are available at special discounts when purchased in bulk quantities
for businesses, associations, institutions, or sales promotions. Please call our Special Sales
Department in New York at (212) 967-8800 or (800) 322-8755.

You can find Chelsea House on the World Wide Web at http://www.chelseahouse.com

Text design by Erik Lindstrom
Cover design by Ben Peterson

Printed in the United States of America

Bang EJB 10 9 8 7 6 5 4 3 2 1

This book is printed on acid-free paper.

All links and Web addresses were checked and verified to be correct at the time
of publication. Because of the dynamic nature of the Web, some addresses and links
may have changed since publication and may no longer be valid.

CONTENTS

1 The Greatest Quarterback Who Never . . .   7

2 Just Walk Down Parkview Avenue   16

3 A Pitt Panther   28

4 Rookie of the Year   42

5 Setting Records   55

6 Frustration and Injury   73

7 A New Era   90

8 After the Cheering Stopped   103

9 In Perspective   113

Statistics   120

Chronology   121

Timeline   122

Glossary   126

Bibliography   133

Further Reading   136

Picture Credits   138

Index   139

About the Author   144

The Greatest Quarterback Who Never . . .

Super Bowl XIX was a football game pitting two of the greatest **quarterbacks** of all time against each other. On January 20, 1985, young Dan Marino led the Miami Dolphins onto the field at Stanford Stadium in Stanford, California, to battle Joe Montana and the San Francisco 49ers.

Marino was only in his second season as a professional quarterback, having graduated from the University of Pittsburgh in 1983. However, he had just completed the greatest year any quarterback had ever had in **National Football League (NFL)** history. That year, Marino had become the first quarterback to throw for more than 5,000 (5,084) **yards** in a season. He also set records for pass completions (362), number of games passing for 300 yards or more (9), and number of games passing for 400 yards or more (4). Most astonishingly, he threw an incredible 48 **touchdown** passes. To put this record in perspective, the previous high mark for touchdown passes in a season was 36 by Houston Oilers quarterback George Blanda (1961) and New York Giants quarterback Y. A. Tittle (1963). The record had not been broken for 20 years, yet Marino smashed it by an incredible 12 touchdown passes. "This boy is in a class by himself," said Tittle. "There is just no denying that."

MAKING A RUN IN THE PLAYOFFS

Behind Marino's leadership, the Dolphins won the AFC East Division and had a 14–2 regular-season record in 1984, the best in the **American Football Conference (AFC)**. In the playoffs, they destroyed the Seattle Seahawks, 31-10, and then crushed the Pittsburgh Steelers in the AFC Championship Game, 45-28. Marino had been superb in these playoff games as well. In the two games, he had passed for 683 yards and seven touchdowns, including 421 yards against the Steelers. These were especially amazing numbers because both of these teams ranked in the top 11 in the NFL in points allowed per game.

Marino's rival in the championship game, Joe Montana, already owned a Super Bowl ring. Montana had been named MVP of Super Bowl XVI in 1982, when San Francisco defeated Cincinnati, 26-21. Montana also had a sensational season in 1984. He threw for 3,630 yards, 28 touchdowns, and only 10 **interceptions**. These were exceptional numbers, although they could not compete with Marino's season.

However, Montana had something that Marino did not yet have. When people talked about Montana, they called him a *clutch* player. Clutch is a word that is hard to define in football. In general, it means to be able to perform under extreme pressure in an important situation. In baseball or basketball, being a clutch performer could often be determined by looking at statistics. "Clutch" was a little harder to define in football. Yet everyone agreed that Montana had that indefinable quality. He

Hall of Fame quarterbacks Joe Montana (left) and Dan Marino pose for a photograph a few days before a preseason football game in London in July 1988. On January 20, 1985, the two met in Super Bowl XIX. On that day, Montana's team, the San Francisco 49ers, got the better of Marino's team, the Miami Dolphins, 38-16.

always seemed to make the big play when his team needed it. San Francisco fans felt confident with the ball in his hands with time running down and the season on the line. The jury was still out on Marino's ability to perform under extreme pressure.

Super Bowl XIX would also be a classic contest between a fantastic offense and a rock-solid defense. San Francisco's defense had allowed the fewest points (227) in the NFL. All four of their **defensive backs**—Dwight Hicks, Ronnie Lott, Carlton Williamson, and Eric Wright—had been selected to play in the Pro Bowl. This defense had helped lead San Francisco to a 15–1 record, the best in the NFL. They would have the responsibility of stopping Marino and Miami. The Dolphins had led the league in scoring with an amazing 513 points (more than 32 points per game). They had scored more than twice as many points as San Francisco had given up. The San Francisco defensive backs knew what they were facing. "You were basically at Dan's mercy," future Hall of Fame defensive back Ronnie Lott told ESPN. "All the great ones see the game so quickly that when everybody else is running around like a chicken with his head cut off, they know exactly where they want to go with the ball. It's like they see everything in slow motion."

All Super Bowls generate excitement. The playoffs in professional baseball, basketball, and hockey end with a best-of-seven game series. Football, however, like soccer, ends with a one-game winner-take-all contest. As a result, there is a huge buildup to the event. Yet even by football standards, Super Bowl XIX began with an air of great anticipation. Which team, which quarterback, would come out on top?

THE GAME

San Francisco received the opening **kickoff**, and the Dolphins quickly forced the 49ers to **punt**. Marino took the field for his first Super Bowl **snap**. Throughout the stadium, people watched in anticipation, wondering how the young quarterback would perform. At first, Marino did not disappoint. He fired a 25-yard completion to **running back** Tony Nathan on his very first play. On this first series, he drove the Dolphins to the 49ers' 20-yard line, where kicker Uwe von Schamann connected on a 37-yard **field goal**. After the 49ers came back to take a 7-3 lead, Marino retaliated with a touchdown **drive** of his own, capped by a two-yard touchdown pass to **tight end** Dan Johnson. At the end of the first quarter, the Dolphins had a 10-7 lead. The game was living up to its billing.

In Miami's previous two playoff games, the Dolphins had run the ball 74 times. In the Super Bowl, however, they called only eight running plays, placing their hopes almost completely on Marino's right arm. Marino had gotten off to an excellent start, completing 9 of his first 10 passes. Coach Don Shula had instructed Marino to call the plays at the **line of scrimmage** without a **huddle** so that the Dolphins could put more pressure on the San Francisco defense.

However, the 49ers countered by adding an extra defensive back and organizing their defense almost entirely against the Dolphins' pass attack. The 49ers' defense started to pressure Marino and shut down his receivers. The game began to turn. In the second quarter, the wheels came off for Miami. The 49ers scored three touchdowns to take a 28-16 lead into halftime.

Any possibility of a Dolphins comeback quickly disappeared during the first few minutes of the second half. Miami received the kickoff, but the 49ers **sacked** Marino on third down of the first series. After Miami punted, Montana led the 49ers down the field to their fifth touchdown and a commanding 35-16 lead. In the end, San Francisco crushed the Dolphins, 38-16. Marino was sacked four times, the most in a year in which he had only been sacked 13 times all season. After the game, Marino said, "We knew what we had to do but they took us right out of our game." Don Shula put it even more simply. "We were dominated," said the coach.

Marino had had a decent game but not a great one. He completed 29 of 50 passes for 318 yards and a touchdown. However, Marino also threw two interceptions deep in 49ers territory, and he was responsible for the game's only **fumble**.

On the other hand, San Francisco finished the game setting a number of Super Bowl records, including most yards gained (537). Montana, who won his second Super Bowl MVP Award, set a Super Bowl record for passing yardage by a quarterback (331). He had completed 24 of 35 passes for three touchdowns. He even ran for another touchdown.

Montana had won the battle of the great quarterbacks. Yet after the game, Marino could afford to shrug his shoulders.

After all, he was only 23 years old and had just finished his second season in the NFL. He was on a solid team with one of the best coaches in the game. The future looked bright for Marino and the Dolphins. He figured there would be many more Super Bowls in the years to come.

Year after year, Marino continued to shine. He racked up awesome passing statistics. He achieved many personal milestones. With his powerful right arm and incredibly quick release, Marino shaped the way professional football was played during the 1980s and 1990s. He helped switch the emphasis from the run to the pass.

However, there would be no championship for Marino or the Dolphins. In fact, he never reached the Super Bowl again. His battle with Montana at 23 would be his first and last trip to the Super Bowl in a career that spanned 17 seasons, all with the Dolphins. He would get married, have children, and adopt children. He would raise millions of dollars for charity and start his own charitable foundation. He would be an iron man who never missed a game during his first 10 seasons and then a hobbling quarterback with no mobility during the last few years of his career. Eight playoff victories and 10 playoff defeats would come and go. There would be no Super Bowl ring for Marino.

In every sport, there is a club that no player wants to join. It is not an official club, but one that is recognized by sportswriters and sports fans. The club is "The Greatest Players Never to Win a Championship" in a particular sport. Players such as Boston Red Sox outfielder Ted Williams and longtime Detroit Tigers outfielder Ty Cobb in Major League Baseball, or Utah Jazz forward Karl Malone and forward Charles Barkley, who played for the Philadelphia 76ers, Phoenix Suns, and Houston Rockets, in the National Basketball Association are members of the club. They had stellar careers, but whether through some fault of their own or just plain bad luck, they never won a championship.

In football, the quarterback has more influence on the game than any other player. The quarterback is oftentimes

A dejected Dan Marino paces the sidelines shortly before the end of Super Bowl XIX. During his career, Marino was never able to win a Super Bowl, which, to this day, still haunts the former NFL MVP.

cheered the most when the game is won. However, because the quarterback has such a prominent role, he often has to face criticism. When the game is lost, the quarterback is often blamed. John Elway of the Denver Broncos was the losing starting quarterback in three different Super Bowls. People questioned his performances in clutch situations. Then, at the end of his career, he was the winning quarterback of Super Bowl XXXII in 1998 and Super Bowl XXXIII in 1999. No one doubted his abilities under pressure after he finally won the big game. He had broken free from the nonchampions club. Marino said, "When John Elway won his first Super Bowl in

1998 after chasing it for as long as I had, my eyes misted up when he held that trophy over his head. I was that happy for him, that touched by the scene. I was jealous, too. I'll regret not knowing what he felt that day, walking off that last football field of the season a winner."

For Marino, that moment of redemption never came. When he finally retired after the 1999 season, he owned just about every NFL passing record of significance. He held the record for career pass completions (4,967), passing yards (61,361), and touchdown passes (420). However, as Marino himself noted, "Football is a team game, and losing takes away from the records. Every record I've set has been in a game we've lost. It's hard to appreciate them. . . . I've set a lot of records. I've had a great career. But I haven't won a Super Bowl."

DEFINING A CHAMPION

In a simpler time, famous sportswriter Grantland Rice had said that it was "not that you won or lost but how you played the game." However, sports in modern America is a huge business. Professional football generates billions of dollars and attracts millions of spectators. In the modern football era, the more famous quote belongs to former Green Bay Packers coach Vince Lombardi, who stated the following: "Winning isn't everything; it's the only thing." In the United States, champions are revered as true competitors, while losers are often labeled as not being up to the challenge.

Where does this leave Dan Marino? Is his career fatally flawed because he could not fulfill Lombardi's vision of being a champion and winning a Super Bowl? Or is Lombardi's opinion exactly what is wrong with competitive sports in the United States today?

At the end of his career, Marino was asked about what winning a Super Bowl would mean to him. Marino said, "I want to win a Super Bowl. But at this point, I don't think failing to win one is going to take away from what I have accomplished on the football field. You gain a certain respect for consistency, work ethic, and whatever you are able to accomplish because of those things."

Nonetheless, many people consider Marino's career incomplete. Of the 23 modern quarterbacks (since 1945) in the Pro Football Hall of Fame (as of 2007), only six had never won a Super Bowl: Dan Fouts (San Diego Chargers), Sonny Jurgensen (Philadelphia Eagles and Washington Redskins), Jim Kelly (Buffalo Bills; four Super Bowl appearances), Fran Tarkenton (Minnesota Vikings; three Super Bowl appearances), Warren Moon (Houston Oilers; five Canadian Football League championships), and Y. A. Tittle (Baltimore Colts, San Francisco 49ers, and New York Giants; three NFL championship games). Only Fouts and Jurgensen have fewer team accomplishments than Marino. Whether it matters or not, Marino is undoubtedly the greatest quarterback who never won a Super Bowl.

However, this is not the end of the story. One or even a number of games cannot sum up a man's life. In 2005, Marino reflected on his 17 seasons in a Miami Dolphins uniform. "Looking back on my career I've accomplished many things," he said. "But what I cherish more than any record that I hold, any fourth-quarter comeback, any win that I was involved in, [are] the relationships that I've made, the people I've worked with, the teammates I've lined up beside and the opponents that I've competed against. But friends and family, that's what I cherish most."

Just Walk Down Parkview Avenue

Daniel Constantine Marino Jr. was born on September 15, 1961, in Pittsburgh, Pennsylvania. He grew up on Parkview Avenue in the South Oakland section of the city with his father, Dan Sr.; his mother, Veronica; and his younger sisters, Debbie and Cindi. Veronica's side of the family came from Poland, but Dan Sr.'s father came to Pittsburgh from Italy. He worked in a steel mill in the area until he was killed in an accident when he was just 27 years old. Dan Sr. was born in South Oakland and lived there all his life.

The neighborhood where Marino grew up would have an enormous impact on his life. Oakland is about three miles east of the downtown Pittsburgh central business district. During his acceptance speech into the Pro Football Hall of Fame in 2005, Marino would say,

My dream started right there on Parkview Avenue in Oakland and it stayed there for 21 years. There's not many players who can say they went to grade school, high school, college all in the same neighborhood, all within a short walk from the home that I grew up in. It was literally a 10-minute walk from my home to the 50-yard line of old Pitt Stadium.

OAKLAND

Pittsburgh's Oakland neighborhood is large and has several different sections. North Oakland—an area vaguely defined as between Neville and Bouquet streets—includes major sections of the University of Pittsburgh and many retail stores on Craig Street. South Oakland, where Marino grew up, is a more residential area with one boundary along the Monongahela River. Parkview Avenue has a sweeping view of Schenley Park, Pittsburgh's best-known park, founded in 1889 from a large donation of land by former resident Mary Schenley.

North Oakland is Pittsburgh's cultural, medical, and educational center. Andrew Carnegie selected the area for a library, museum, lecture hall, and technical school around 1900. Forbes Field, the old home of the Pittsburgh Pirates baseball team, was built in Oakland in 1909. At the turn of the twentieth century, local entrepreneur Frank Nicola attracted the University of Pittsburgh (which was then located in the city's North Side). In the 1920s, Oakland became part of an urban design trend called the "City Beautiful" movement; the University of Pittsburgh's 42-story Gothic revival Cathedral of Learning, one of the world's tallest educational buildings, was completed in 1937. North Oakland became known for art museums, universities, architecture, entertainment, and general hustle and bustle.

Dan Marino's neighborhood of South Oakland was nothing like this. Outside of the cultural hub, Oakland's residential areas grew with almost no planning at all. The hills, bluffs, and

Dan Marino grew up in the South Oakland section of Pittsburgh; a neighborhood primarily made up of working-class residents who had immigrated from Italy and eastern European countries a generation or two before. This sign on Dawson Street illustrates that Marino was not the only famous resident of this section of Pittsburgh; pop artist Andy Warhol also grew up in this neighborhood, three decades before Marino.

valleys became home to middle- and working-class residents, including immigrants from Greece, Italy, and most eastern European countries. By 1950, 22,000 people lived in Oakland.

Earlier in the century, many of the immigrants of South Oakland had worked in the enormous Jones & Laughlin steel mill. The mill was located below the bluff on which the community sits, overlooking the Monongahela River. By the time Marino was born, the Pittsburgh steel industry was in decline. Many area residents still had blue-collar jobs but not factory work. Some worked in Oakland's educational and cultural institutions or in the sports stadiums located in the neighborhood. Few people in this working-class neighborhood owned a car. Oakland residents took it for granted that a person got around by bus and/or foot.

PLAYING FOOTBALL AS A KID

Marino had been throwing footballs in the neighborhood for as long as he could remember. His dad worked as a nighttime delivery driver for a Pittsburgh newspaper. That job left him free in the afternoons to play catch with his son. Dan remembered that he and his father would play at the field at the end of their street: "He'd be waiting for me to get out of school. Then we'd throw to each other the rest of the day." Sometimes the two would play baseball, as Dan Sr. hit him grounders. The games were for fun, but Dan's father also taught him at the same time. These lessons not only included instruction on how to hold the ball and throw it but also the importance of practice and a good work ethic. When Marino was inducted into the Pro Football Hall of Fame in 2005, he said, "As a young man, God blessed me with a special talent to throw a football and I was very fortunate to grow up in an environment like the city of Pittsburgh in the neighborhood of Oakland, an area that was full of football tradition."

Young Dan loved to throw at anything outside his house on Parkview Avenue. Throwing any kind of ball gave him a sense of pure pleasure. Although he played several **positions** in baseball, Dan liked pitcher the best. In football, the local kids always chose him to play quarterback in the neighborhood pickup games. Those games would take place in the streets, and the kids would only stop to let buses and cars drive by.

Like many kids who grow up in the city, the Oakland kids had to adapt the game of football to fit their environment. The streets were too narrow to allow more than four players on a team; the **end zones** would be telephone lines or sewers, and curbs served as the **sidelines**. Parked cars usually were out of bounds, but only if a person touched them. The field could change dramatically if someone moved a parked car. When

Dan could not find enough kids to play a game, he might throw at the telephone poles, pretending cars and buses were opposing **linebackers**. When he was about 10 years old, Dan's father told him, "I think if you work hard, set your mind to it, and are lucky enough to stay healthy, you can become a pretty good athlete."

Marino's neighborhood was filled with second-generation working-class Americans. It was a sports-crazy environment typical of many white ethnic neighborhoods in large cities throughout the country. Dan's grammar school, St. Regis, was located directly across the street from the Marino home. The school had a fifth-grade football team. Dan started out as a water boy for the team in the fourth grade. He then played for the school team from fifth to eighth grades. His mother told the *Pittsburgh Post-Gazette* that, "This one game, he had a concussion, and he actually played the game and then they took him to a hospital. That was really scary because he was so young. You think to yourself, is this good for your child? But, if they want something, how can you stop him?"

Dan was not a particularly good student, though. His sixth-grade teacher told the Marinos that Dan would probably never make it through high school. But Dan really wanted to attend Central Catholic High School, a Pittsburgh football power just a short walk from his home. He attended summer school after eighth grade just to achieve the necessary grades to get into the school. His hard work was rewarded, and he enrolled in the fall of 1975.

PITTSBURGH: THE CRADLE OF QUARTERBACKS

Marino enjoyed his high school years, although Central Catholic was perhaps not as idyllic as Marino remembered it. The school's most famous student was talented playwright August Wilson, the chronicler of Pittsburgh history. Wilson was the only black student in his class at Central Catholic in 1959 and told author George E. Curry that, "There was a note on my desk every single day. It said, 'Go home, nigger.'" Wilson lasted a year before the threats and abuse drove him away.

However, if you were a white football player, the school was much different. In his first year, Dan was the starting quarterback for the freshman team. As a sophomore, he was the **backup** quarterback for the varsity and played on **special teams**. He then started every game for Central Catholic in his junior and senior years. Marino not only played quarterback but also was the punter and placekicker. In one game, he threw three touchdown passes and kicked an **extra point**, as his team won, 19-18. His football coach, Rich Erdelyi, built the Central Catholic offense around Marino's arm. Most high school teams run the ball far more than they pass it. But at Central Catholic, it was the opposite. In one game, Marino threw the ball on 39 of Central Catholic's 55 offensive plays (completing 17 passes).

Years later, Marino reminisced that, "When I was a kid sometimes the most competitive games I played were in the neighborhood in the street, the street games. [Pittsburgh] is a great city to grow up in. It's an area that just loves football. High school football there is as good as it gets anywhere. I will always have ties, relationships in that city. It is very special to me."

Marino grew up in the right region because people in the Pittsburgh area love football. From the 1910s to the 1940s, schools such as the University of Pittsburgh, Duquesne University, Carnegie Tech (now Carnegie Mellon University), and Washington and Jefferson College all made bowl game appearances and ranked high in the national polls. Although the University of Pittsburgh, which is commonly referred to as "Pitt," is the only school in the group that still plays major college football, local residents also rooted for the professional Pittsburgh Steelers. Dan Marino grew up a Steelers fan during the years of the team's greatest success—the Steelers won four Super Bowls in the 1970s while Marino was a teenager. When he was 15 years old, in 1976, the University of Pittsburgh won the **National Collegiate Athletic Association (NCAA)** championship in football. These were exciting times to be a boy growing up in Pittsburgh who loved football.

Western Pennsylvania is sometimes known as the "cradle of quarterbacks." Some of the greatest quarterbacks in football history—Johnny Unitas (Baltimore Colts), Joe Namath (New York Jets), George Blanda, Joe Montana, and Jim Kelly—have come from western Pennsylvania. The area has produced many other quarterbacks who have played in the NFL, such as Johnny Lujack, Bruce Gradkowski, Gus Frerotte, Chuck Fusina, Charlie Batch, Marc Bulger (a Central Catholic graduate), and the modern NFL's first black quarterback, Willie Thrower. No one really knows why western Pennsylvania keeps producing talented quarterbacks. It just does.

As a kid, Marino used to dream of becoming the next Joe Namath. Namath was born and raised in Beaver Falls, a steel town about 30 miles northwest of Pittsburgh. When Marino was seven years old, Namath led the New York Jets to a shocking 16-7 victory over the Baltimore Colts in Super Bowl III. Namath was famous for perhaps having the quickest release of any quarterback in NFL history. As a kid, Marino liked to read Namath's book, *A Matter of Style*. Ironically, when he reached the NFL, Marino would constantly be compared to Namath for his quick release and strong arm.

Growing up in Pittsburgh, Marino also was influenced by the charismatic Steelers quarterback Terry Bradshaw. Between 1975 and 1980, Bradshaw led the Steelers to four Super Bowl titles. What made Bradshaw particularly admirable was his ability to excel in big games. During his career, Bradshaw passed for more than 300 yards in a game only seven times; Marino would do it 63 times. However, three of Bradshaw's 300-yard games came in the playoffs, two of them in Super Bowls. Marino later remembered, "I loved Bradshaw because I was a Steelers fan growing up right in the city there in Pittsburgh. Bradshaw was my guy."

Former New York Jets quarterback Joe Namath was one of Dan Marino's idols while Marino was growing up in Pittsburgh. Namath is from nearby Beaver Falls and is one of several western Pennsylvania quarterbacks who played in the NFL.

BASEBALL OR FOOTBALL?

Dan Marino's entire world revolved around sports. He saw a professional career in football or baseball as a perfectly achievable goal. During one summer in high school, Marino needed some extra spending money. He took a job cutting grass and pulling weeds for a lawn service. He soon found himself working outside in the heat of the summer for minimal pay. After flipping a lawn mower and nearly cutting off his toes, Marino swore he would not be a manual laborer. Lacking any educational aspirations, he decided that sports would be his ticket to success. However, he would have to choose: Should he put his energies into baseball or football?

Marino was a superb baseball player. He pitched and played shortstop, both positions that favored his strong arm. His fastball was once clocked at 92 miles per hour, an exceptional speed for a high school player. He compiled a 22–0 record in three years as a pitcher at Central Catholic. Playing shortstop and outfield when not on the mound, Marino hit .513 as a senior with a .987 slugging percentage.

It was in youth baseball that Marino wore the number 13 for the first time. Many people think 13 is an unlucky number. However, number 13 was the last large jersey left when Marino was playing American Legion baseball. Marino was not superstitious, and he gradually came to like the number. He ended up wearing number 13 for the rest of his sports career.

In June 1979, at the end of Marino's senior year, Major League Baseball's Kansas City Royals drafted him in the fourth round. (Ironically, in the eighteenth round of the same draft, the Royals chose John Elway.) The Royals wanted Marino to play third base or the outfield and offered him a $35,000 contract. As a high school graduate, Marino had to decide between college football and professional baseball. The NCAA had just changed the rules to allow players to compete as an amateur in one sport and play professionally in another. Marino briefly considered doing that. However, if a person chose to do it that way, he could not accept a scholarship. Instead, the athlete would have to make enough money in the pros to offset the cost of college tuition.

In the end, Marino's decision was almost purely financial. If he played baseball, he would have to pay tuition and live somewhere else while he played in the minor leagues. This would eat up almost all of the $35,000. So Marino turned down the Royals and decided to give up baseball completely and put all his energies into playing football at a high-profile college.

Marino's stellar play on the football field had not gone unnoticed. By the fall of his senior year in 1978, Marino was named to several All-American teams. Recruiting letters

During the mid-1970s, future NFL Hall of Fame running back Tony Dorsett helped lead the University of Pittsburgh back to national prominence on the gridiron. Dorsett is pictured here during the Panthers' 27-3 win over the Georgia Bulldogs in the 1977 Sugar Bowl. That season, the Panthers won the national title, and Dorsett rushed for 1,948 yards and 23 touchdowns to win the Heisman Trophy.

poured in from many major football programs. Dan visited Clemson, Florida State, and Arizona State. He thought long and hard about possibly going to school in California. He was attracted by the celebrity lifestyle as well as the warm and sunny weather.

However, in the end, Marino was unwilling to leave Pittsburgh. He remembered walking the few blocks to Pitt Stadium to attend games. He remembered watching Tony Dorsett lead Pitt to the national championship in 1976. Two weeks before having to make his final decision, Marino called University of Pittsburgh defensive coordinator Serafino "Foge" Fazio on the phone to set up a meeting. Fazio recruited Marino by simply reminding him that he was a Pittsburgh kind of guy. Fazio said, "I just told him what he would mean to the program and reminded him of where he came from."

Marino explained his choice the same way: "All those times I played football in the streets, I would look up and see the Cathedral of Learning. Something, maybe my heart, told me to stay home and go to Pitt." However, he also admitted in

ANOTHER FAMOUS OAKLAND RESIDENT: ANDY WARHOL

Dan Marino was not the only notable person to grow up in the South Oakland neighborhood of Pittsburgh. Andy Warhol, the world-famous artist, was born in Pittsburgh in 1928 and grew up at 3252 Dawson Street in South Oakland. His parents came from the Carpathian Mountains in what is now Slovakia. Warhol, born Andrej Warhola, attended Pittsburgh's public schools and went to Saturday morning art classes at Carnegie Institute. Because Warhol was a sickly child and not good in sports, kids in South Oakland picked on him. While Warhol recovered from various ailments, he used to draw, listen to the radio, and collect pictures of movie stars. Warhol later credited this period of his life in Pittsburgh with influencing his preferences and sharpening his skills. At the age of 17, he was accepted at Carnegie Institute of Technology (now Carnegie Mellon University). From there, he moved to New York City and a career as one of the most important artists of the twentieth century. The Andy Warhol Museum opened in Pittsburgh in 1994.

his autobiography that, by staying at Pitt, he could "dump off laundry with Mom, have the occasional dinner at home, and still play in one of the nation's best programs."

By the late 1970s, the Pittsburgh of Marino's youth was changing. The steel industry had disintegrated, bringing massive layoffs. The once-mighty (and sooty) ironworks that stretched along the Monongahela River near Oakland were closing down. Second- and third-generation residents were moving to the suburbs or out of state. Pittsburgh's population dropped from 677,000 in 1950 to 424,000 by 1980. South Oakland was now filled with elderly homeowners and short-term student renters. Already, the Oakland of Marino's childhood was becoming a memory. Yet, in later years, he would say in his autobiography, "If you want to understand who I am and what I became, just walk down the Parkview Avenue of my youth."

A Pitt Panther

When Dan Marino began his career at the University of Pittsburgh in 1979, the school already had a long and glorious football history. Pitt's first football team had been organized as early as 1889. For almost a century, Pittsburgh residents had enjoyed watching games against rivals such as Penn State, Notre Dame, and Syracuse. In recent memory, fans had watched All-Americans such as tight end Mike Ditka (1958–1960). However, the Panthers, as they were known, had not been particularly successful in football in the 1960s.

In 1973, two men arrived at the Oakland campus to change that situation. Johnny Majors, previously the coach at Iowa State, became Pitt's 26th head coach. In addition, Tony Dorsett, a 5-11, 192-pound running back from nearby Aliquippa, Pennsylvania, enrolled as a freshman. In Majors's first game as head coach, Dorsett ran for 100 yards and Pitt stunned the University of Georgia with a 7-7 tie at Georgia's Sanford Stadium. A new era had begun. In Dorsett's first season, Pitt made its first bowl appearance since 1956. As a junior, he ran for an amazing school-record 303 yards on just 23 carries, as the Panthers defeated Notre Dame, 34-20. It was Pittsburgh's first victory against Notre Dame since 1963.

THE GOLDEN ERA OF PITT FOOTBALL

Marino's college years were part of a new golden era of University of Pittsburgh football. The pinnacle was reached in 1976, before Marino even set foot on campus. That year, Tony Dorsett became the NCAA's all-time rushing yardage leader and won the Heisman Trophy, which recognizes the best college football player in the nation. Pitt went undefeated, winning all 11 of its regular-season games. In the Sugar Bowl, Dorsett ran for 202 yards, and quarterback Matt Cavanaugh passed for one touchdown and ran for another to win the game's MVP Award. The Panthers' 27-3 victory over Georgia earned Pitt the NCAA national championship in football. It was the Panthers' first major bowl appearance since 1955, their first national championship since 1937, and their first unbeaten and untied season since 1917.

Johnny Majors had worked some magic during his four years at Pitt. He inherited a football program that had gone 1–10 in 1972 and guided it to a 33–13–1 record. In 1976, Majors was named national coach of the year but decided to leave Pitt to become head coach at Tennessee, his alma mater. Dorsett ended his four-year career with 6,082 rushing yards and 356 points, both NCAA records at the time.

Majors was replaced by his assistant, Jackie Sherrill. Sherrill had become famous at Pittsburgh for recruiting Tony Dorsett. When Dorsett was a shy high school senior, Sherrill visited

Dorsett's house three times a week for six straight months in order to have Dorsett commit to Pitt. Now, Dorsett was gone, and Sherrill was the coach. In his five seasons at Pittsburgh, Sherrill's Panthers would go 50–9–1.

When Marino arrived as a freshman in 1979, Coach Sherrill was amazed as he watched Marino work out. After

BREAKING GROUND

University of Pittsburgh football also was famous for its commitment to promoting civil rights. In 1945, Jimmy Joe Robinson became the first African-American to suit up for the Panthers. At the time, he was one of only a few dozen black players on major college football teams. Then, in 1956, Bobby Grier became the first African-American player to break the laws of segregation at the Sugar Bowl in New Orleans, Louisiana. The game took place only one month after Rosa Parks refused to give up her bus seat for a white man in Montgomery, Alabama.

Pittsburgh (7–3) was scheduled to play Georgia Tech (9–1–1). However, Georgia governor Marvin Griffin urged Georgia Tech to skip the game because Pitt had a black player. A black football player had never played in the Sugar Bowl. Governor Griffin told the State Board of Regents that, "The South stands at Armageddon. . . . We cannot make the slightest concession to the enemy."

Most white people, even in the South, were embarrassed by the governor's position. Almost 2,000 Georgia Tech students marched to the governor's mansion and hung Griffin in effigy. However, some Georgia Tech alumni, as well as white citizens of New Orleans, fought to prevent Grier or Pittsburgh from playing in the Sugar Bowl.

practice, he asked the young quarterback who taught him how to throw. When Marino told him it was his dad, Sherrill responded, "Listen to me. Whatever you do, don't let anyone tell you to do anything different. Just keep doing exactly what you're doing." Sherrill would later say that this was one of his all-time best coaching tips.

University of Pittsburgh officials refused to back down. They said Pitt would play only if Grier, a **fullback** and linebacker, could play and if the sections of Pitt fans were not racially segregated. "We all got together and voted not to go to the Sugar Bowl if Bobby Grier was not allowed to play," said Bob Rosborough, a **wide receiver** for Pitt. "He was one of us and we would rather not play than leave one of ours behind." Many Georgia Tech athletes agreed. Tech's quarterback, Wade Mitchell, said he considered the entire situation "silly."

To Governor Griffin's displeasure, the Georgia Board of Regents voted 10–1 to allow the team to participate. However, they did forbid any future college games in the state of Georgia between integrated teams. This prohibition was never enforced.

Ironically, Pittsburgh lost the Sugar Bowl, 7–0; a controversial penalty against Grier led to the Georgia Tech touchdown. Grier later served in the U.S. Air Force and then as an administrator at a Pittsburgh community college. Fifty years later, Grier reminisced, "It all seems so long ago. We've all come a long way. But when you think about it, you still have to wonder what in the world the fuss was all about."

In 1979, Marino's first year in college, Pitt lost to North Carolina, 17-7, in the second game of the season. However, the Panthers then won nine games in a row to finish the regular season 10–1. Marino made an appearance in the season opener against Kansas. His very first collegiate pass was an interception. This would rattle some first-year quarterbacks but not Marino. His third pass was for a touchdown. By midway through his first season, Marino had become the Panthers' starting quarterback. The last win of the season came on Christmas Day, when Pitt defeated Arizona, 16-10, in the Fiesta Bowl in Tempe, Arizona, to finish 11–1. Marino threw a touchdown pass, but kicker Mark Schubert's three field goals earned him MVP honors.

Rick Trocano, the Panthers' other quarterback, faced a dilemma before Marino's sophomore season. Trocano realized he would have a tough time winning the starting job back. He had been Pitt's starting quarterback in 1978, completing 138 of 283 passes for 1,648 yards and 5 touchdowns. But "the writing was on the wall," Trocano said, "and I can read. Marino was going to be the quarterback and I was going to sit on the bench." Rather than play backup quarterback, Trocano volunteered to play defensive back. In that way, Marino became the undisputed starting quarterback as a sophomore.

Trocano adjusted well to his new position. He became part of a fearsome defensive unit led by Hugh Green, a dominating **defensive end** and the best lineman in college football. Green was so good, he almost won the Heisman Trophy, finishing second to South Carolina running back George Rogers in 1980. That same year, the Panthers led the nation in rushing and total defense. Pitt won its first four games before losing, 36-22, to Florida State on a hot and humid October night in Tallahassee. In the next game against West Virginia, Marino suffered a twisted left knee. Trocano, now playing **safety**, got the chance to fill in. Pittsburgh's offense had no trouble adapting to their old quarterback and won, 42-14.

Dan Marino became Pitt's starting quarterback midway through his freshman season and led the Panthers to an 11–1 record, which included a 16-10 win over Arizona in the Fiesta Bowl. Marino is pictured here rolling out of the pocket during the Panthers' 28-21 win over Syracuse on November 3 of that year.

Pitt finished the 1980 season with an 11–1 record and ranked second in the nation. Longtime Florida State head coach Bobby Bowden, who has seen many great players and great teams, later remarked, "I've said it many times, in all my years of coaching, that Pitt team was the best college football team I have ever seen."

If nothing else, the 1980 University of Pittsburgh roster was one of the greatest collections of talent ever to play together on one college team. All 22 **starters** were drafted into the NFL. From the defensive unit, all five linemen (Hugh Green, Rickey Jackson, Greg Meisner, Bill Neill, and Jerry Boyarsky) started in the NFL, as did three of the defensive backs (Carlton Williamson, Lynn Thomas, and Tom Flynn). On offense, all five linemen (Jimbo Covert, Mark May, Russ Grimm, Rob Fada, and Ron Sams) started in the NFL, as did the receivers (Julius Dawkins and Dwight Collins), the quarterback (Dan Marino), the fullback (Randy McMillan), and the kicker (Dave Trout). Five underclassmen also went on to start in the NFL, and many other members of the team played professional football in the United States or in Canada. Pitt outscored its opposition, 380–130, in 1980. In one game at Syracuse, the defense held running back Joe Morris, who had broken the school rushing records of Jim Brown, Ernie Davis, and Larry Csonka, to 12 yards on 16 carries.

In the 1980 Gator Bowl against South Carolina, Pitt's two quarterbacks split playing time. The Pitt defense had something to prove because South Carolina was led by running back George Rogers, the Heisman Trophy winner. Although Rogers gained 113 yards on 27 carries in the game, it was 59 yards below his season average. Trocano finished his career with one of his best performances, as he ran for one touchdown, passed for another, and completed 10 of 21 passes for 155 yards. Trocano also brilliantly directed Pitt's ball-control offense that kept Rogers off the field for large parts of the game. Marino chipped in, completing 7 of 13 passes for 78 yards and a touchdown, as Pitt easily defeated South Carolina, 37-9. Trocano was named MVP of the Gator Bowl, a happy conclusion for a young man who thought he would never play quarterback again.

For the second year in a row, Pitt finished the season with just one loss. However, Georgia, led by running back Herschel Walker, won the national championship by beating Notre Dame, 17-10, in the Sugar Bowl. Pittsburgh had only lost that one game against Florida State, but Georgia had gone undefeated. There could be no argument as to which team was number one.

Marino's best season in college was his junior year in 1981. With Trocano having graduated, Coach Sherrill opened up the offense to take advantage of Marino's rifle arm, quick release, and self-confidence. Marino had a spectacular year. He led the NCAA with 37 touchdown passes. He also passed for 2,876 yards, with a nearly 60 percent completion rate. Pittsburgh finished 11–1 for the third straight year. Unfortunately, Marino was doomed to face disappointment once again in his quest for a national championship.

At one time or another during the 1981 season, six different teams were ranked number one in the college polls. It seemed as if no one wanted the top spot. Michigan was the preseason pick but lost its opening game to Wisconsin. Notre Dame moved up but quickly lost to Arizona. Texas took over and was promptly destroyed by 31 points by Arkansas. Penn State, Pitt's archrival, was next to be promoted, but the Nittany Lions lost to Miami.

Everything seemed perfectly set up for Marino and the University of Pittsburgh. They had won their first 10 games and had only Penn State left at home and then a bowl game. Then, the unthinkable happened. With the national title on the line, Penn State annihilated Pittsburgh, 48-14, to ruin the Panthers' chance at a national title. The beginning of the game gave no hint as to its outcome. Marino had led Pitt to scoring drives on the Panthers' first two possessions. By the end of the first quarter, Marino had completed 9 of 10 passes for 117 yards and two touchdowns, and Pitt led its nemesis, 14-0. Then the roof fell in. Marino threw a couple of interceptions, and Penn State scored 48 unanswered points. It was one of the lowest moments in Pittsburgh football history.

Nonetheless, Pitt played in another high-profile bowl game. In the 1982 Sugar Bowl, Marino and Pitt faced Georgia, the previous year's national champion. Georgia still had an outside chance to win another national title, but Pitt and Marino saved their best game for last. The Panthers' defense held Heisman Trophy runner-up Herschel Walker to 84 yards rushing on 25 carries. After five lead changes, Pitt was behind

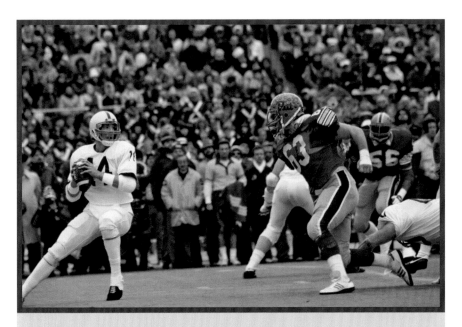

During Dan Marino's junior season in 1981, the Panthers got off to a 10–0 start and were ranked number one in the country. Unfortunately, their hopes of winning the national championship were dashed by Penn State, 48-14, in the last game of the regular season. Here, Penn State quarterback Todd Blackledge drops back to pass during the Nittany Lions' stunning victory over the Panthers at Pitt Stadium.

by three points late in the fourth quarter. The Panthers had the ball and faced a fourth-and-five, at the Georgia 33-yard line. The Pittsburgh players convinced Coach Sherrill to go for the **first down** instead of attempting a long field goal for the tie. Georgia **blitzed**, but Pitt's backs picked it up. Marino hit tight end John Brown with a perfect 33-yard touchdown pass with 42 seconds remaining to give the Panthers a 24-20 victory. "You fantasize about great last-second comebacks when you're playing on the schoolyard," Marino told ESPN.com years later, "but this was for real."

It was Pitt's seventh consecutive year in a bowl game and the team's sixth victory during that span. But after the bowl games were finished, Clemson had won the national championship by going 11–0 and beating Nebraska in the Orange Bowl, 22-15. However, Marino's great year led to a fourth-place finish in the Heisman Trophy voting. This was a huge honor for a college junior.

HEISMAN TROPHY VOTING—1981

	PLAYER	COLLEGE	CLASS	POSITION	NO. OF VOTES
1	Marcus Allen	USC	Senior	Running back	1,797
2	Herschel Walker	Georgia	Soph.	Running back	1,199
3	Jim McMahon	BYU	Senior	Quarterback	706
4	Dan Marino	Pittsburgh	Junior	Quarterback	256
5	Art Schlichter	Ohio State	Senior	Quarterback	149

A DISAPPOINTING SENIOR SEASON

Expectations were riding high for Pitt football heading into the 1982 season. The Panthers had finished the 1981 season ranked fourth in the Associated Press poll. The team seemed poised to win a national championship, and Marino, now a senior, was the favorite to win the Heisman Trophy. In Marino's first three seasons at Pitt, the team had been 33–3.

However, Marino's senior year turned out to be a huge disappointment. Pittsburgh was not terrible—they finished 9–3—but the preseason hype turned out to be unjustified, as Marino threw more interceptions than touchdowns (23 to 17). "The bottom fell out my senior year at Pittsburgh," Marino later observed. "It's never fun to play poorly or to be questioned. It certainly wasn't for me that senior year at Pitt. But I think it served me well to learn how to handle everything that came with the game's ups and downs. Some people call it growing another layer of skin. I just call it growing up."

Problems arose before the season even started. Marino's two favorite receivers, tight end John Brown and wide receiver Julius Dawkins, had both graduated. In addition, Jackie Sherrill had left Pitt to become head coach at Texas A&M. He was replaced by the team's defensive coordinator, Serafino "Foge" Fazio. Fazio had played football at the University of Pittsburgh and then coached high school football in western Pennsylvania. Fazio and Pitt seemed to be a perfect match, but the honeymoon would not last long.

The Panthers began the season with seven straight victories and looked poised to win the national championship. However, the team simply did not come together. They were crushed by Notre Dame at home, 31-16, and also lost their last game of the regular season to archrival Penn State, 19-10. Marino said in his autobiography, "Nothing went right. It was the first time I struggled, the first time people doubted my game, and the only time other than my final Dolphins season that I threw more interceptions than touchdowns."

Pittsburgh was still selected to play in the Cotton Bowl against Southern Methodist University (SMU). SMU was the nation's only unbeaten team at 10–0–1, yet was ranked fourth because of a weaker schedule. They had a pair of great running backs in Eric Dickerson and Craig James, who were known as the Pony Express. Pitt was 9–2 and ranked sixth in the nation. SMU needed to win by a large margin to win the national title.

Marino's last game as Pitt's quarterback was played in a light rain and 38°F (3°C) weather. Unlike the previous year's bowl game, this was not one of Marino's better efforts. In an amazing first quarter, Pitt opened the contest driving 71 yards to the SMU 1-yard line, only to lose the ball on a fumble. SMU then marched all the way back to the Panthers' 7-yard line on a drive that took nearly 10 minutes, but they also fumbled. Pitt led 3-0 heading into the final quarter, but then SMU scored with 13:43 to play. There was plenty of time for Marino to lead the comeback. He moved Pittsburgh

After leading Pitt to a 9–3 record during Dan Marino's senior season in 1982, Head Coach Serafino "Foge" Fazio struggled to keep the Panthers among the nation's elite teams. The Panthers posted a winning record in 1983, but then won just eight games during the next two seasons. Fazio (right) is pictured here with Penn State coach Joe Paterno before their game in 1983.

to the SMU 7-yard line. On third down, he **scrambled** to his right, hurried his throw, and was intercepted in the end zone. Marino finished the game completing 19 of 37 passes with 1 interception and 181 passing yards. It was a good but not outstanding game. In comparison, SMU quarterback Lance McIlhenny only attempted 8 passes during the whole game. But Pittsburgh was held to its lowest point total in 89 games, since Navy beat the Panthers, 17-0, in 1975.

SMU got the victory but only by a 7-3 margin. It was enough to earn undefeated SMU the number-two spot in the polls and make their fans bitter for years. To make matters worse for Pitt fans, Penn State ended up winning the national championship. They faced top-ranked and undefeated Georgia in the Sugar Bowl in a number 1 vs. number 2 matchup. Penn State led from the start and upset Heisman Trophy winner Herschel Walker and Georgia, 27–23.

Marino's years at the University of Pittsburgh had certainly been a success. He finished his collegiate career holding every major passing record in school history, including career marks for passing yards (8,597) and completions (693). Twenty-five years after his final collegiate season, Marino still holds Pittsburgh records for touchdown passes in a career (79) and season (37), as well as consecutive games with a touchdown pass (19). These were remarkable statistics for college football, which, at the time, was more of a run-oriented game than today. More important, the Panthers had gone 42–6 during Marino's years at Pitt. Yet there was something vaguely unsatisfying about the experience. Each year, one little thing had gone wrong to keep them from winning the national championship. Despite not winning a national title, three straight years at 11–1 was an astonishing record. Yet Marino's senior season had been the worst of the lot, just when everyone expected him to shine the brightest.

Marino's last season also was the end of the University of Pittsburgh's golden era of football. During the next three seasons, the Panthers would only have a record of 16–15–3, which

DAN MARINO'S YEARS AT THE UNIVERSITY OF PITTSBURGH

YEAR	RECORD	BOWL	AP RANK	UPI RANK	POINTS SCORED	POINTS ALLOWED
1979	11–1–0	W-Fiesta Bowl	7	6	291	116
1980	11–1–0	W-Gator Bowl	2	2	380	130
1981	11–1–0	W-Sugar Bowl	4	2	385	160
1982	9–3–0	L-Cotton Bowl	10	9	300	129
Totals	42–6–0	3–1	—	—	1,356	535

DAN MARINO'S STATISTICS AT PITT

YEAR	ATTS.	COMP.	PCT.	YDS.	TD	INT.
1979	222	130	.586	1,680	10	9
1980	224	116	.518	1,609	15	14
1981	380	226	.595	2,876	37	23
1982	378	221	.584	2,432	17	23
Totals	1,204	693	.576	8,597	79	69

resulted in Coach Fazio being fired after the 1985 season. In the 26 seasons between 1982 and 2007, the Panthers would not have a single season in which they lost fewer than three games and only two seasons (1982 and 2002) when they won nine games. Pitt would not play in another major bowl game until 2004, when it won the Big East Conference with an 8–4 record, but lost, 35-7, to Utah in the Fiesta Bowl. In addition, the Panthers lost seven of their 10 bowl games during this stretch, some by lopsided scores. They would only be ranked in the Top 20 at the end of the season three times and never higher than seventeenth. The days of glory were over.

But Dan Marino would always have fond memories of his hometown school. Returning after his NFL career was over, he told a Pittsburgh crowd that, "I have so many memories here. I have friends and family here, and I grew up here, so it is very special to come back here and be honored. I think the fact that I am in the College Football Hall of Fame speaks to the number of great players we had back then."

Rookie of the Year

Dan Marino's senior year at the University of Pittsburgh had not been a disaster but he had seemed to take a step backwards. One professional football scout wrote in October 1982 that, "Marino is 6-foot-3 5/8, 213 pounds and ran the 40-yard dash in 4.89. . . . Not having a good year, played poorly in the opening game in North Carolina. . . . Marino has an amazing ability to anticipate pass rushers and is able to move side to side to avoid being sacked. . . . He also has one of the quickest releases that I have ever seen and has very good accuracy. . . . I cannot understand why he's had a season that has not been up to what was expected of him."

In the Heisman Trophy voting, Marino only finished ninth behind seven other seniors and winner Herschel Walker (a junior). Four quarterbacks finished above him. An excellent performance in the Senior Bowl, a postseason all-star game, seemed to boost his stock a bit. Marino threw for 178 yards and two second-half touchdown passes to lead the North to a 14-6 win. If nothing else, Marino received a car for winning the game's Offensive MVP Award.

A LONG DAY

As Marino prepared for the April NFL draft, he was presented with another option that was worth looking into. A new professional football league, the United States Football League (USFL), had formed in 1982 to compete with the NFL. USFL officials decided that their best bet at competing with the NFL was to play their games during the spring and summer and, when possible, attempt to sign players who played college football in the same region as the team that drafted them. The Los Angeles Express, a USFL team, made Marino the league's top draft pick in January 1983. Marino was shocked, especially when they offered him $800,000 to sign with them. As Marino

HEISMAN TROPHY VOTING—1982

	PLAYER	COLLEGE	CLASS	POSITION	NO. OF VOTES
1	Herschel Walker	Georgia	Junior	Running back	1,926
2	John Elway	Stanford	Senior	Quarterback	1,231
3	Eric Dickerson	SMU	Senior	Running back	465
4	Anthony Carter	Michigan	Senior	Wide receiver	142
5	Dave Rimington	Nebraska	Senior	Center	137
6	Todd Blackledge	Penn State	Senior	Quarterback	108
7	Tom Ramsey	UCLA	Senior	Quarterback	65
8	Tony Eason	Illinois	Senior	Quarterback	60
9	Dan Marino	Pittsburgh	Senior	Quarterback	47

remembered in his autobiography, this "was big money. Huge money for my family. But as a top NFL pick I'd make more, in an established league, on the kind of stage I'd been dreaming of all my life." So Marino passed on the USFL's offer and geared up for the NFL draft.

Despite his subpar senior season, most people still expected Marino to be selected as one of the top 10 picks in the NFL draft. Marino had played four years at a major college program. He helped lead his team to a 42–6 record. He had excellent size for a quarterback. Yet 26 players, five of them quarterbacks, were selected before Marino. In fact, he was only the third University of Pittsburgh player chosen in the draft; offensive **tackle** Jim Covert was the sixth pick, and **cornerback** Tim Lewis went eleventh.

Marino stayed at home on draft day with his family and some friends. They could only watch in disbelief as team after team passed on the talented quarterback. The Kansas City Chiefs had worked out Marino but decided to take Penn State quarterback Todd Blackledge with the seventh pick instead. The Buffalo Bills took Jim Kelly at number 14. The New England Patriots selected Tony Eason at number 15. As Marino sat at home, he began to become frustrated and confused. His father told him, "Look, no matter what happens, you know you can play, and you know you're as good as any of these guys picked ahead of you. You'll have your opportunity to prove it."

Marino was especially hurt when Pittsburgh chose not to take him with the twenty-first pick. The Steelers passed on their hometown quarterback and took speedy **defensive tackle** Gabriel Rivera from Texas Tech instead. In October of his rookie season, Rivera was almost killed in an automobile accident that left him permanently paralyzed from mid-chest down. During the coming years, Pittsburgh owner Art Rooney would always make a point to speak to Marino when the two teams played and say something about how the Steelers should have chosen him.

After 26 teams passed on Dan Marino, the Miami Dolphins and Head Coach Don Shula eagerly snatched him up with the twenty-seventh overall pick of the 1983 NFL draft. Shula, who is pictured here with Marino during an offensive meeting at training camp, was shocked that the future Hall of Famer was available when it was Miami's turn to pick.

The next possibility was the New York Jets, who had the twenty-fourth pick. They had just talked to Marino the day before the draft and suggested they would take him if he was available. They did pick a quarterback, but it was little-known Ken O'Brien from the University of California-Davis, a Division II school.

The Miami Dolphins had the twenty-seventh selection, the next-to-last pick of the first round. The Dolphins had such a low draft choice because they had played in the Super Bowl the year before. Their coach, Don Shula, had been

ROUND 1 OF THE 1983 NFL DRAFT

Pick	NFL Team	Name	Position	College
1	Baltimore Colts	John Elway	Quarterback	Stanford
2	Los Angeles Rams	Eric Dickerson	Running back	SMU
3	Seattle Seahawks	Curt Warner	Running back	Penn State
4	Denver Broncos	Chris Hinton	Offensive line	Northwestern
5	San Diego Chargers	Billy Ray Smith	Linebacker	Arkansas
6	Chicago Bears	Jim Covert	Offensive line	Pittsburgh
7	Kansas City Chiefs	Todd Blackledge	Quarterback	Penn State
8	Philadelphia Eagles	Michael Haddix	Running back	Mississippi State
9	Houston Oilers	Bruce Matthews	Offensive line	USC
10	New York Giants	Terry Kinard	Defensive back	Clemson
11	Green Bay Packers	Tim Lewis	Cornerback	Pittsburgh
12	Buffalo Bills	Tony Hunter	Tight end	Notre Dame
13	Detroit Lions	James Jones	Fullback	Florida
14	Buffalo Bills	Jim Kelly	Quarterback	Miami (Florida)
15	New England Patriots	Tony Eason	Quarterback	Illinois
16	Atlanta Falcons	Mike Pitts	Defensive end	Alabama
17	St. Louis Cardinals	Leonard Smith	Cornerback	McNeese State
18	Chicago Bears	Willie Gault	Wide receiver	Tennessee
19	Minnesota Vikings	Joey Browner	Defensive back	USC
20	San Diego Chargers	Gary Anderson	Running back	Arkansas
21	Pittsburgh Steelers	Gabriel Rivera	Defensive tackle	Texas Tech
22	San Diego Chargers	Gill Byrd	Cornerback	San Jose State
23	Dallas Cowboys	Jim Jeffcoat	Defensive end	Arizona State
24	New York Jets	Ken O'Brien	Quarterback	UC-Davis
25	Cincinnati Bengals	Dave Rimington	Center	Nebraska
26	Los Angeles Raiders	Don Mosebar	Offensive line	USC
27	Miami Dolphins	Dan Marino	Quarterback	Pittsburgh
28	Washington Redskins	Darrell Green	Cornerback	Texas A&M-Kingsville

(Names in brown indicate player made at least one Pro Bowl appearance in the NFL) impressed by Marino. However, the team's personnel staff had told him there was no chance Marino would be available. Shula called Marino three minutes before the Dolphins had to make their selection to ask Marino if he was interested in playing for Miami. "You bet," Marino responded, and the Dolphins would have the cornerstone upon which they could build their franchise. Shula later remembered, "I really didn't give Marino much thought. I never really dreamed we'd get a shot at him, but when he was there, I wasn't about to let him get away. . . . Picking Marino was one of the easiest decisions I've ever had to make."

The 1983 NFL draft became known as the "Draft of Quarterbacks." Of the six quarterbacks selected in the first round, four played in the Super Bowl and three were inducted into the Pro Football Hall of Fame. (The next highest number of quarterbacks taken in the first round was five in the 1999 draft, and the quality was nowhere near as good.) During the next 16 years, the AFC would be represented in the Super Bowl 11 times by a quarterback taken in this draft.

Years later, at his enshrinement into the Pro Football Hall of Fame, Marino admitted, "I've always been asked the question, did it bother me that twenty-six teams passed on me in the first round. I always answered no. Well, I lied."

A NEW BEGINNING

Marino was thrilled to play for the Miami Dolphins. He quickly signed a contract that would pay him $2 million over four years. He signed another contract to endorse a brand of athletic shoes. Then he went out and bought a new invention, a satellite dish, for his family's home in Pittsburgh. That way, his parents and sisters could watch all the Dolphins games on television. He bought himself a stereo and rented a two-bedroom condominium on Hollywood Beach, near Miami. Marino now had everything he felt he needed in life.

Of course, Marino missed Pittsburgh and his friends from the city. The small triangle of St. Regis, Central Catholic, and then the University of Pittsburgh had made up his entire world

A STORIED HISTORY

Like the University of Pittsburgh, the Miami Dolphins also have a proud, though much shorter, football history. Miami began as an American Football League (AFL) expansion team in 1966. The NFL and AFL merged in 1970, and the Dolphins played in their first Super Bowl a year later (Super Bowl VI). In 1972, the Dolphins went undefeated to post the NFL's first perfect season in the modern era. They won all 14 regular-season games, two playoff games, and Super Bowl VII, a 14-7 win against the Washington Redskins. The team also won Super Bowl VIII, defeating the Minnesota Vikings, 24-7, to become the first team to appear in three consecutive Super Bowls. In 1972–1973, the team had an amazing 32–2 record. Six future Hall of Fame members played for Miami during the 1970s, including running back Larry Csonka, quarterback Bob Griese, middle linebacker Nick Buoniconti, and offensive linemen Jim Langer and Larry Little. When they needed a big-play receiver, the incomparable Paul Warfield was available.

Don Shula became the Dolphins' head coach in 1970 and would lead them for the next 26 years. By the end of his career, Shula was the winningest head coach in NFL history with 347 victories. The consistency of Shula's teams was extraordinary. His Dolphins teams posted losing records in only two of his 26 seasons with the club.

until he arrived in Miami. He had played 12 years of school and college ball in places no more than 15 minutes apart. However, Marino came to enjoy the South Florida lifestyle. He liked the weather and the beach. He drove around in a flashy car and endorsed products for local clothing stores.

Marino also lucked out by being drafted by an organization that had a winning tradition. The Dolphins were not a desperate team, and Marino did not have to be their savior. After all, the Dolphins were the defending AFC Champions and had lost to the Washington Redskins in the Super Bowl. They had a tough offensive line anchored by **center** Dwight Stephenson, as well as Pro Bowl **guards** Bob Kuechenberg and Ed Newman. They had other offensive stars such as running back Tony Nathan and wide receiver Nat Moore. They also boasted an exceptional defense known as the Killer B's, taken from many of their last names: defensive linemen Doug Betters, Bob Baumhower, and Bill Barnett; linebackers Kim Bokamper and Bob Brudzinski; and the Blackwood brothers (Glenn and Lyle, both safeties). If Marino played, he would not be a sitting duck in the **pocket**. Marino later observed in his autobiography, "Little did I know then it was the best collection of talent I'd ever be around in the pros."

Shula had been extremely successful with the Dolphins of the 1970s using a ball-control offense and a strong defense. That was now ancient history. The Dolphins of 1982 were missing a top-notch quarterback. In 1980, David Woodley had taken over for Bob Griese, who severely injured his shoulder in a game against the Baltimore Colts. Griese never recovered from the injury and retired after that season. For the next two years, Shula alternated between Woodley and Don Strock as quarterback in a system popularly known as "Woodstrock." It had obviously worked well enough, because the Dolphins went to the Super Bowl after the 1982 season. However, the Dolphins' passing attack ranked last in the league that year

Miami Dolphins quarterback Dan Marino jokes around with his teammates on the first day of training camp in July 1983. From the start, the Dolphins knew that they had drafted a talented quarterback—by the sixth game of his rookie season, Marino had become the team's starting quarterback.

with just 1,401 total yards, 8 touchdowns, and 13 interceptions. These were pathetic statistics for a championship team.

In the Super Bowl, the Washington Redskins exposed Miami's weakness at quarterback. Woodley started well with a 76-yard touchdown pass but struggled as the game went on. Washington completely dominated Miami in the second half, allowing only two first downs. Woodley did not complete a pass in eight attempts in the second half, and the Redskins scored 17 unanswered points to beat Miami, 27-17. Overall, the Dolphins' offense had just nine first downs and four pass completions in the entire game. Woodley finished the game 4 of 14 for 97 yards, 76 of which came on his first pass.

For this reason, Shula was thrilled to be able to draft Marino, supposedly as his quarterback of the future. Shula said, "When we brought Dan to camp as a rookie, everyone saw his talent. . . . The difference [between Marino and Woodley] was startling. . . . [Woodley] was an NFL talent who quarterbacked the Dolphins to the Super Bowl the previous year. But practice sessions . . . underlined what a singular talent Dan was right from the start." The Dolphins' veterans noticed it also. Tony Nathan was a small but superb running back who excelled at catching passes. Nathan remembered, "The first time you saw him throw the football, or the first time you actually caught one of those balls, it was like OK he's OK—he's got a little ways to go; he's an arrogant young man. . . . You know, he was a raw individual, but you knew he could throw the football."

Marino was determined to succeed. He would later write in his autobiography that, "My disappointing senior season, the unsettling draft, the critics, the questions, all of it served one purpose. It assured I would be in the best shape possible for my first training camp. I worked my butt off that summer in hope of making a good first impression." He did not lack for confidence. One of his trademark sayings was, "I've never seen the harm in dreaming big dreams as long as you're willing to work toward them."

He also was aided by the relationship he developed with quarterback Don Strock. Strock had played at Virginia Tech and led the nation in total passing and total offense in 1972. He had just helped lead the Dolphins to the Super Bowl. Yet the 10-year veteran was perfectly willing to help teach Marino what he knew about playing quarterback in the NFL. Strock was particularly impressed by Marino's willingness to listen and learn, not always common traits for a rookie. The two became lifelong friends to the point that Marino's kids would call Strock "Uncle Don." Marino later noted that, "As a quarterback I couldn't have had a better teammate to learn from or a better friend."

ROOKIE SEASON

Marino began his rookie season at Miami as the backup quarterback to David Woodley. However, Woodley played poorly in the first few games of the season. Marino appeared in his first NFL game on September 19, 1983, four days after his twenty-second birthday. The Los Angeles Raiders were beating the Dolphins 27-0 in the fourth quarter when Coach Shula decided to give his rookie quarterback a look. Marino threw his first completion, a nine-yard pass, to second-year wide receiver Mark Duper. He followed that with his first touchdown pass (six yards) to tight end Joe Rose. Marino completed two touchdown passes in the last three minutes of the game, making the final score 27-14.

After five games, the defending AFC Champion Dolphins were only 3–2. On October 9, Shula awarded Marino his first start against Buffalo in the sixth game of the season. Miami fell behind 14-0, but in the second half, Marino completed 14 of 20 passes for 268 yards and 3 touchdowns. Miami eventually lost 38-35 in overtime. However, it was the 35 points that caught everyone's eye. Duper had 7 catches for 202 yards and 2 touchdowns in the loss, while rookie wide receiver Mark Clayton had 2 catches for 53 yards and a touchdown. The Dolphins franchise was on the verge of a new offensive era, one in which the passing attack took precedence.

In only one of the first five games of the 1983 season had Miami scored more than 14 points. After the Buffalo game, the Dolphins would score 20 points or more in every game except one. In Marino's next start against the New York Jets, the rookie quarterback hit wide receiver Nat Moore for a 66-yard touchdown pass less than three minutes into the game. He threw two more touchdown passes, and the Dolphins won,

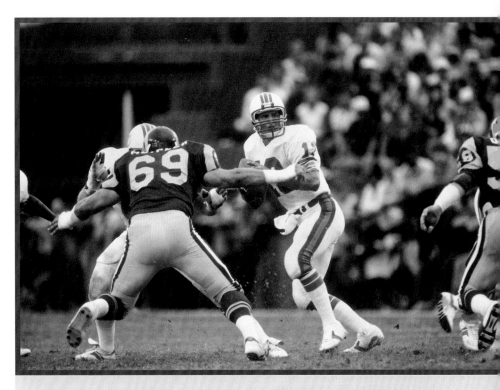

In 11 games during his rookie season, Dan Marino passed for more than 2,200 yards and 20 touchdowns. His stellar play allowed him to become the first rookie in NFL history to start in the Pro Bowl. Here, Marino drops back to pass against the Los Angeles Rams, a game the Dolphins won, 30-14.

32-14. Bob Kuechenberg, Miami's All-Pro guard, remembered a moment from that Jets game:

> I was on the sideline, taking a breather. We were inside their 30 and Marino had the ball, trying to look down-field with this defensive lineman in his face. I was standing next to Don Shula, and I blinked my eyes and from the ball being in front of him with a guy in his face, it was in the end zone to [tight end] Joe Rose. In the blink of an eye! I thought, "Did I really see that?" I glanced at Shula. He had the same look.

Marino made the job of quarterback look easy. After the loss to the Bills, the team won every game but one under Marino's leadership. Marino was almost unstoppable and set a host of rookie quarterback records. In 11 games, he completed 173 of 296 passes for 2,210 yards, threw 20 touchdown passes, and only had 6 interceptions (17 fewer than his senior season in college!). Marino led the Dolphins to the AFC East Division title and a 12–4 record. The Dolphins seemed to be a completely different team; they scored 38 points against the Bengals and put up 37 against the Colts. Thanks to his quick release and the Dolphins' strong offensive line, Marino was only sacked 10 times. Jim Jensen, one of Marino's receivers, said, "The amount of time where he sees his target and then his mind tells him to throw it is a short span. He sees it; it's gone. There's no thinking."

However, just when many people began to assume Miami would return to the Super Bowl, they were upset at home in the divisional round of the playoffs by the Seattle Seahawks, 27-20. Marino had a good game but not a great one. He completed 15 of 25 passes for 193 yards and two touchdowns in the second quarter. However, he also threw two key interceptions after only throwing six the entire season.

Despite the disappointment of losing in the playoffs, Marino won the NFL Rookie of the Year Award. He was the first rookie since the merger in 1970 to lead a conference in passing. He also became the first rookie quarterback selected as a starter in the Pro Bowl. In February 1984, the Dolphins traded David Woodley to the Pittsburgh Steelers. The job of starting quarterback for the Miami Dolphins would belong to Dan Marino for the next 16 years.

Setting Records

Coach Don Shula had achieved enormous success in Miami with a defense-first philosophy and a ball-control offense. The great Dolphins teams of the 1970s had been famous for the strong running of Larry Csonka, Eugene "Mercury" Morris, and Jim Kiick.

After Dan Marino's great rookie year, however, Shula decided to change his strategy. He felt he had the best young quarterback in the NFL; why not take advantage of his skills? For the next 16 seasons, Miami would be known as a team with an average rushing game, an erratic defense, and a lethal quarterback. The Dolphins often talked about establishing a running game in those years, but they never seemed to develop a premier running back. However, as Coach Shula noted, a football team had to play to its strength: "Dan's passing was

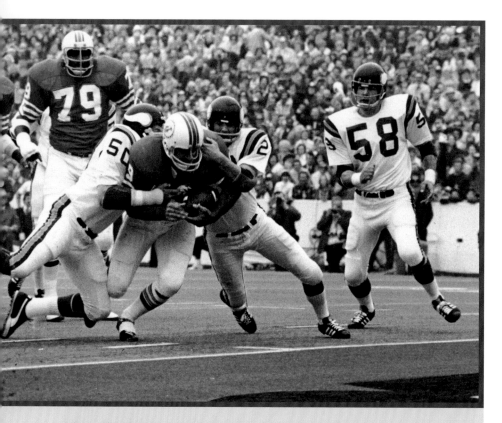

Prior to Dan Marino's arrival in 1983, the Dolphins were primarily a run-oriented team. Miami's stable of running backs included All-Pros Larry Csonka and Eugene "Mercury" Morris, each of whom rushed for more than 1,000 yards in the Dolphins' perfect season of 1972. Here, Csonka scores a touchdown in Miami's 24-7 win over the Minnesota Vikings in Super Bowl VIII.

the kind of strength you didn't strategically stray from. You couldn't. At least not if you wanted to win."

Years later, running back Tony Nathan was asked if he thought Shula had been "too pass happy" with Marino. Nathan replied, "Well, we did throw it a lot more than we had in the past before Marino got there. It's one of those deals where, yes, I thought we did, but maybe he [Shula] didn't think so because he was putting the ball in the best talent's hands and it was up to somebody else to come through for him and help him out."

A NEW NFL

Marino's career, and Shula's new strategy, were both aided by changes in the NFL rules that Shula himself had helped to write. Shula served continuously on the NFL competition committee from 1975 until his retirement after the 1995 season. During that time, the committee adopted sweeping rule changes to add action, tempo, and especially scoring to football games.

During the mid- to late 1970s, the Pittsburgh Steelers had dominated the NFL, winning four Super Bowls behind their intimidating "Steel Curtain" defense. In Super Bowl IX, in 1975, the Steelers' defense limited the Minnesota Vikings to just 17 rushing yards in a 16-6 victory. In the last nine games of the 1976 season, the Steelers gave up a total of just 28 points. In 1978, the Steelers held their opponents to an NFL-low 195 points and won their third Super Bowl.

NFL officials were concerned. Scoring production had reached its lowest point in football's post-World War II era. The NFL knew that its fans liked offense; many Americans disliked soccer, mainly because there was not enough scoring and there were not enough play stoppages for television viewers to go to the refrigerator. Football's share of the television audience was now far more important to team owners than the traditions of the game or the people who went to see it live. Everyone knew that defense usually won championships; the Steelers had demonstrated it yet again. However, defense did not bring in casual television viewers who would buy products advertised during the games. The NFL was determined to surpass baseball as America's sport and make vast amounts of money in television contracts. To do that, they needed to make it harder to play defense and easier to throw the ball. In other words, they needed to change the rules.

Football was not unique in this strategy. Basketball had reacted to the chants of "Defense" by New York Knicks fans in Madison Square Garden by reinstating the dunk in the mid-1970s. This opened the door for acrobatic performers such as Julius Erving and David Thompson and, later, Michael Jordan. Baseball had reacted to the dominance established by pitchers in the 1960s by altering its rules to help hitters. The NHL was about to shift into the high-scoring Wayne Gretzky years of the 1980s. Americans wanted to see home runs and slap shots, not hit-and-runs and neutral-zone traps.

For example, in football in the early 1970s, a cornerback could hit a wide receiver at any point on the field. Many of the wide receivers could not handle that kind of pounding. In 1977, the NFL changed the rules so that defenders could make contact with eligible receivers only once. In the same year, the competition committee made it illegal for a defensive lineman to strike an opponent above the shoulders or to use a head slap. Before that rule was instituted, defensive linemen could freely use their arms and hands as weapons to get past offensive linemen. Now offensive linemen would not have to tuck their heads and duck when they were pass **blocking**; although they, in turn, could no longer thrust their hands to a defensive lineman's neck, face, or head. The following year, defenders were outlawed from making contact with a receiver once he got five yards past the line of scrimmage.

In 1979, the NFL instituted a rule change to protect quarterbacks. Quarterbacks were usually the most marketable and famous players on a football team. In an often faceless sport, they were almost always white and appeared to be in charge. This appealed to television viewers who did not want to see the stars lost to injury and then have to watch backup quarterbacks play. Therefore, the committee ruled that the referee should whistle the play dead [over] once a quarterback was clearly in the grasp of a tackler. This ensured that the marquee quarterbacks were not pulverized.

The changes in the late 1970s worked. By Marino's second season in professional football, a CBS Sports/*New York Times* survey reported that 53 percent of the nation's sports fans said they most enjoyed watching football compared to 18 percent for baseball. In 1984, NFL teams would combine to average 42.4 points per game, the second-highest total since the 1970 merger.

A RECORD-BREAKING SEASON

Dan Marino's rookie season of 1983 was fantastic, but the next year was even better. In 1984, Marino had one of the greatest seasons for a quarterback in NFL history. He set several passing records, including touchdowns (48), passing yards (5,084), and completions (362). He became the first NFL quarterback to throw for more than 5,000 yards in a season. He also set the record for number of games passing for 300 yards or more (9) and number of games passing for 400 yards or more (4). Marino's feats left NFL coaches and players gasping in amazement. "What Dan accomplished is to have a better season than anyone who has ever played this game," said Hall of Fame quarterback Roger Staubach. "I'm talking about quarterbacks, wide receivers or anyone else. He was unbelievable."

Marino was greatly helped by his gifted receivers. The two most famous were Mark Duper and Mark Clayton. Together the pair became known as the "Marks Brothers." Years later, when Marino was inducted into the Pro Football Hall of Fame, he said,

> I wish I could thank all of you individually, but I would like to mention a few. Two guys—Mark Duper and Mark Clayton. . . . In 1984, we set a standard for throwing the football that teams are still trying to match today. And the one thing I remember most about Duper and Clayton is their competitive spirit and their attitude that they were the best. Every time they would come back to the huddle, they would always insist that they were open and that they always wanted the ball.

Wide receivers Mark Duper (left) and Mark Clayton were Dan Marino's two favorite targets during the majority of his career with the Dolphins. Both receivers played with Marino from 1983 through 1992 and combined for more than 1,000 receptions.

And they constantly reminded me that they were making me a star. Thank you, guys.

Clayton, from the University of Louisville, was a rookie with Marino on the 1983 Dolphins. He would make the Pro Bowl five times and finish his 11-year career with 582 **receptions**, 8,974 receiving yards, and 84 touchdowns. Marino later said in his autobiography, "Right from the first practices, maybe because as rookies we practiced together more, Mark Clayton and I made that intangible and indescribable connection that great passing combinations have. He knew what I sensed. I saw what he did. We also had similarly fiery on-field personalities."

Mark Duper, Marino's other favorite target, had blazing speed (4.3 seconds in the 40-yard dash) and was almost as prolific. He was drafted from Northwestern State University in Louisiana the year before Marino and Clayton. Duper played 11 seasons for the Dolphins and caught 511 passes for 8,869 yards and 59 touchdowns. Later in his career, he would legally change his name to "Mark Super Duper."

In addition to the "Marks Brothers," Marino had other sure-handed receivers such as Jim Jensen, Tony Nathan, Nat Moore, and Jimmy Cefalo. In later years, his favorite target would be O. J. McDuffie. Marino did not hold it against McDuffie that he went to Penn State; in 1998, McDuffie caught 90 passes to lead the NFL. As of 2007, he is the only Dolphins player ever to achieve this feat.

When the 1984 season began, some people wondered if Marino's rookie season was a fluke. But Marino was confident. Looking back, he said, "We thought Clayton might win a starting job in 1984. We did some extra work together in the off-season. We were all young, and we thought, as a group, we might be able to do some pretty good things." Indeed, Marino's

DAN MARINO'S CAREER COMPLETIONS BY RECEIVER

(100 catches minimum)

1	Mark Clayton	538		10	Tony Paige	140
2	Mark Duper	492		11	Tony Martin	136
3	O. J. McDuffie	336		12	Bernie Parmalee	124
4	Tony Nathan	222		13	Lorenzo Hampton	121
5	Jim Jensen	217		14	Ferrell Edmunds	112
6	Bruce Hardy	167		15	Keith Jackson	112
7	Troy Stradford	157		16	Keith Byars	109
8	Nat Moore	153		17	Troy Drayton	107
9	Irving Fryar	146				

confidence often bordered on arrogance. During the season, he said, "You go out there with the thought in mind that you're going to score every time you get your hands on the ball. If you don't think that way, why even go out there?"

In a season in which Marino averaged an amazing three touchdown passes per game, it is hard to pick a game that stands out above the others. In the season opener against the Washington Redskins, he completed 21 of 28 passes for 311 yards, five touchdowns, and no interceptions or sacks in a 35-17 win. Against the St. Louis Cardinals, in the fifth game of the season, Marino passed for 429 yards and three touchdowns to lead the Dolphins to a 36-28 victory. He tied the NFL record for most touchdown passes (36) in a season when he threw for four in a 28-17 win against the New York Jets—and there were still three games to go in the season. He threw four touchdown passes in each of his last three games to end up with 48 for the season. In the final game of the regular season, Marino hit Clayton for touchdown passes of 39, 41, and 83 yards, as the Dolphins beat the Dallas Cowboys, 28-21.

As the season progressed, Marino also became known for his seemingly magical ability to avoid being sacked. Film of Marino during his high school days actually shows him running the ball, but by the time he reached the Dolphins, he was strictly a pocket passer. Marino was not fleet of foot; in 301 total career rushing attempts, he averaged less than one yard per carry. During his 17-year career, Marino never had more than 18 rushing yards in a single game or a run longer than 15 yards.

Despite his slowness, Marino was rarely sacked. Several factors accounted for this. Throughout his career, the Dolphins had an excellent pass-blocking offensive line. Marino had a whiplike quick release, and because of his size, he was not easy to bring down. However, he also possessed an amazing awareness in the pocket, often shuffling a step or two to the left or right to avoid the pass rush. Against a decent

New England Patriots team in 1984, the Dolphins tied their franchise record by racking up 552 yards; Marino threw for 316 yards and four touchdowns with no sacks in the 44-24 win. New England defensive end Doug Rogers was mystified: "We should have had four or five sacks today. How does a guy like that escape, as big as he is?" In fact, Marino was only sacked 13 times during the 1984 regular season and not once in the first two playoff games.

By the time the 1984 season ended, Marino was not the only Dolphins player who had posted some astronomical numbers. Duper had 71 catches, 1,306 yards receiving, and 8 touchdowns. Clayton caught 18 touchdown passes, which, as of 2007, is tied for the third-highest total in NFL history. In addition, Marino was named NFL Player of the Year for 1984.

In the playoffs, the Dolphins destroyed the Seattle Seahawks, 31-10. The Dolphins ran 70 plays, gained 405 yards of total offense, and scored 17 unanswered points in the second half. Marino threw three touchdown passes, including a 33-yarder to Mark Clayton and a 34-yard pass to Jimmy Cefalo.

Marino's Dolphins would also be victorious in the AFC Championship Game for the only time in his career, as they defeated the Pittsburgh Steelers, 45-28. Marino had an amazing game, throwing for 421 yards and four touchdowns (and one interception). Duper finished the game with five receptions for 148 yards and two touchdowns. Clayton caught four passes for 95 yards and a touchdown. Nathan ran for 61 yards and a touchdown, while also catching eight passes for 114 yards. At the end of his career, Marino called his touchdown pass to Duper the favorite moment of his career: "It worked perfect all week in practice and it worked perfect in the game. When those things happen, it is very special."

The Miami offense seemed unstoppable. Pittsburgh defensive coordinator Tony Dungy said after the AFC title game that, "Marino knows right away who the open man will be and he'll shoot it in there, and Duper and Clayton are really dangerous against a zone. They'll catch the ball in the middle of the field and make one tackler miss, and then they'll run a long way."

With the win, the Dolphins were going to their fifth Super Bowl in 15 seasons. No one knew then that it would be the first and last of Marino's career. Years after the 49ers defeated

IN THE TRENCHES

Offensive linemen in football are perhaps the most underappreciated players in any major sport. Guards, tackles, and centers earn their money by making plays that few fans notice. They have no statistics to justify their worth. Yet no offense can succeed without them.

The great Dolphins teams of the 1970s had one of the best offensive lines of all time: Hall of Famers Jim Langer and Larry Little, along with Pro Bowlers Wayne Moore, Bob Kuechenberg, and Norm Evans. However, the offensive linemen on the 1984 team were also superb: Hall of Fame center Dwight Stephenson, Pro Bowler Ed Newman, and Roy Foster, Jon Geisler, Cleveland Green, Jeff Toews, and Ronnie Lee.

Stephenson was the heart of the offense. Marino later called him "the best center to ever play the game of football." Stephenson was voted an All-Pro five consecutive times from 1983 to 1987. Marino said, "Because of what I had to concentrate on during a game, it was hard for me to notice Dwight while he was in there. But I sure noticed it when he was not in there."

Anchored by Stephenson, the Dolphins' offensive line gave up the least quarterback sacks in the NFL for a record six the Dolphins, 38-16, in Super Bowl XIX, Marino would look back ruefully:

> We were having so much fun and I think a lot of people didn't anticipate how good our offense was. It seems like it was so easy, a lot easier than it is now. But I don't think we understood what it was all about. I was twenty-three years

straight seasons, from 1982 to 1987. Stephenson's career ended in 1987, when he severely injured his knee after being chop blocked by New York Jets defensive tackle Marty Lyons on a fumble return. "I have no bitterness towards Marty Lyons," said Stephenson. "I know he didn't mean it."

After Stephenson retired, the Dolphins' line continued to protect Marino brilliantly. They extended the least quarterback sacks record to nine straight seasons, tripling the length of the previous record. In the 1990s, Richmond Webb led the Dolphins' offensive line, setting team records for 118 consecutive starts and seven consecutive Pro Bowls. With his golden arm and lightning-quick release, Marino would go on to set several NFL records, including career touchdown passes (420), passing yardage (61,361), and completions (4,967). But he could not have done it without his offensive line.

MOST CONSECUTIVE SEASONS LEADING LEAGUE, FEWEST TIMES SACKED

9	Miami, 1982–1990
3	St. Louis, 1974–1976
2	By many teams

In 1984, Dan Marino had one of the best statistical seasons in NFL history when he set six league records, including passing yards (5,084) and touchdowns (48). He was not only named NFL MVP, but he helped lead the Dolphins to a 14–2 regular-season record and an appearance in Super Bowl XIX.

old. We felt we could do it every year. It's probably one of the reasons we got beat in the Super Bowl. We didn't take it as seriously as we should have. We didn't understand what it took to get there. You just have to take advantage of it, because you may not ever get that chance again.

PRESERVING HISTORY

The next season, 1985, Miami finished 12–4 and won the AFC East Division title for the third straight year. Marino had another fine season, but the moment that was remembered by most fans occurred on the night of December 2. That night, the 8–4 Dolphins were set to face the 12–0 Chicago Bears on Monday Night Football. In their previous two games, the Bears had shut out the Dallas Cowboys and the Atlanta Falcons. It seemed likely that the Bears would become the first team since Don Shula's 1972 Dolphins to go through a season undefeated.

The Bears had an unusual "46 Defense" that used a variety of different blitz schemes. Most teams kept extra blockers in to protect against the blitz and had trouble moving the ball. Shula did the opposite. The Dolphins tried to take advantage of Marino's unbelievably quick release by spreading the field with four receivers. He wanted the Dolphins' receivers to go one-on-one with Chicago's defensive backs. On the Dolphins' first possession, Marino hit Nat Moore for a 33-yard touchdown pass. It was the first touchdown scored against the Bears' defense in 14 quarters. It would not be the last. In the second quarter, a 52-yard completion by Marino set up another touchdown, and then, after a blocked punt, Marino hit Moore for a six-yard touchdown. The Dolphins scored 31 points in the first half *alone* against one of the best defenses in NFL history. Shula later said it was the best half of offense he had ever seen in all his years in the NFL. Marino finished the game with three touchdown passes and the Dolphins won, 38-24. They were the only team that beat the 15–1 Chicago Bears that season. In the Bears' last six games of the season, not counting the game against Miami, they gave up only 33 points total!

The victory against Chicago made most Miami fans believe that the team would return to the Super Bowl. In the divisional round of the playoffs, in Miami, the Dolphins trailed the Cleveland Browns, 21-3, in the third quarter and the home fans began to boo. Then Marino went to work. The Dolphins scored 21 unanswered points—the final touchdown with 1:57 left to play and won, 24-21.

Many people were looking forward to a rematch between Miami and Chicago in Super Bowl XX. However, the underdog New England Patriots, the Dolphins' AFC East Division rival, had different ideas. New England forced six Dolphins **turnovers** and won, 31-14, in the AFC Championship Game. It was the Patriots' first win in Miami since 1966—New England had lost an astonishing 18 games in a row at the Orange Bowl. Tony Eason, New England's quarterback, had been chosen ahead of Marino in the 1983 NFL draft. Eason now seemed to justify his worth. He only attempted 12 passes in the game, but it was the Patriots who would advance to the Super Bowl against the Bears. (Unfortunately for the Patriots, the Bears won, 46-10.)

THE BEGINNING OF A DROUGHT

While Marino would never have another year like 1984, he had a sensational season in 1986. He threw for 4,746 yards and 44 touchdowns. Not until St. Louis Rams quarterback Kurt Warner threw 41 touchdown passes in 1999 did another quarterback even reach 40 touchdown passes in a season. Marino finished the year as the AFC's top-rated passer. He led the NFL in yards and touchdowns and set records for completions (378) and passing attempts (623).

The season also was notable as the year when the Jets-Dolphins rivalry reached fever pitch. Ever since the NFL merger in 1970, the Dolphins and the Jets have both been in the AFC East Division and have met twice every year. No matter what their records are at the time, the games are almost always competitive. The New England Patriots and the Buffalo Bills are also in the AFC East Division, but there was always something a little special when the Jets met the Dolphins. The two teams have played a number of classic games.

The most important meeting between the two teams took place the year before Marino joined the Dolphins. In the 1983 AFC Championship Game, the two teams battled on a ridiculously muddy field for the right to play in Super Bowl XVII.

During their NFL careers, Dan Marino and Jets quarterback Ken O'Brien played in several thrilling contests against each other. Perhaps the most memorable took place on September 21, 1986, when each quarterback passed for more than 400 yards. Here, O'Brien throws downfield in the Jets' 51-45 overtime win.

This "Mud Bowl" featured 10 turnovers, including eight interceptions, before the Dolphins won, 14-0.

The rivalry intensified in that off-season after the 1983 NFL draft. The Jets had the twenty-fourth pick and had the chance to take Marino but instead chose Ken O'Brien from UC-Davis. O'Brien would go on to have a fine 11-year career: He passed for more than 25,000 yards, led the Jets to three playoff appearances, and earned two Pro Bowl invitations. Some of O'Brien's greatest games were against the Dolphins.

At the same time, Marino threw for at least three touchdowns in more than half of his games against the Jets. During his 17-year career, he threw an incredible 72 touchdown passes versus the Jets.

The most memorable Marino/O'Brien duel came on September 21, 1986. When the dust had settled, the two young quarterbacks had combined to set NFL single-game records of 884 net passing yards and 10 touchdown passes, records that still stand in 2007. Marino completed 30 of 50

MEMORABLE GAMES OF THE MIAMI–NEW YORK RIVALRY

DATE	SCORE	NOTEWORTHY
January 23, 1983	Miami 14 New York 0	In the "Mud Bowl," (AFC Championship Game) Dolphins linebacker A. J. Duhe intercepts three Jets passes
November 4, 1984	Miami 31 New York 17	The "Helicopter Catch"—Dolphin Nat Moore takes one of the most dramatic hits of all time but holds on to the ball; Marino throws for 422 yards
November 10, 1985	Miami 21 New York 17	Mark "Super" Duper sets Dolphins' single-game record with 217 receiving yards in his first game back from injury
September 21, 1986	New York 51 Miami 45	Marino and O'Brien combine for 884 net yards passing and 10 touchdowns
November 24, 1986	Miami 45 New York 3	Marino completes 29 of 36 passes, as 5–6 Dolphins stun 10–1 Jets
October 18, 1987	New York 37 Miami 31	In a scab game during the NFL strike, the Dolphins (55) and Jets

passes for 448 yards and six touchdowns; Duper had 154 receiving yards and Clayton 174. Not to be outdone, O'Brien threw for 479 yards and four touchdown passes, all to wide receiver Wesley Walker. One of O'Brien's touchdown passes to Walker came with no time left on the clock, which forced overtime. Then he threw the game winner in overtime for a 51-45 Jets victory.

Marino and the Dolphins would get their revenge two months later. The Jets came to Miami with a 10–1 record (at

DATE	SCORE	NOTEWORTHY
		(49) combine for 104 passing attempts, second highest in NFL history
December 7, 1987	Miami 37 New York 28	All-Pro center Dwight Stephenson's career ends after chop block from the Jets' Marty Lyons
October 23, 1988	New York 44 Miami 30	Marino passes for 521 yards, fourth highest of all time, but also throws five interceptions
December 22, 1991	New York 23 Miami 20	In the last game of season, Jets win and make playoffs; Dolphins lose and go home
November 27, 1994	Miami 28 New York 24	The "Clock Play" game
December 13, 1998	New York 21 Miami 16	Jets linebacker Chad Cascadden picks up a Marino fumble and returns it for a touchdown to give Jets AFC East title
December 27, 1999	New York 38 Miami 31	In his last game against the Jets, Marino passes for 322 yards and three touchdowns
October 23, 2000	New York 40 Miami 37	In the "Monday Night Miracle," the Jets overcome a 30-7 Dolphins lead in the fourth quarter to win in overtime

the time, the best in the NFL), while the Dolphins were 5–6. The Dolphins wound up embarrassing the Jets. Marino completed 29 of 36 passes for 288 yards and four touchdowns in a 45-3 win.

However, the season was not a successful one for the team. The Dolphins stumbled to a 2–5 start. They only finished 8–8 and missed the playoffs for the first time since 1980. It would be the beginning of several years of frustration for the Miami Dolphins and Dan Marino.

Frustration and Injury

When the 1987 season began, Dan Marino had started more than 50 consecutive games for the Dolphins. He was particularly proud of that streak. "There were a lot of tough guys on those Dolphin teams," he remembered, "and I'd like to think I was one of them. You can't play injured, but you had to play hurt. I did that." Quarterbacks play with less padding than most other players. It was highly unusual for a quarterback to play so long without being injured. "The consecutive game thing, I'm really proud of that. Lining up and playing every week—your teammates knowing you're going to be there. The rest of the records just come from playing every week." In fact, Marino started every game for the Dolphins for an entire decade.

THE NFL STRIKE

However, Marino's consecutive start streak for a quarterback is not in the record book. That is because there was a players strike in 1987. The established NFL players went on strike and the owners replaced them for three games with scabs. (A scab is a person who refuses to honor a strike and crosses a picket line in order to work where the strike is taking place.) So Marino found himself walking the picket line in 1987, while so-called "replacement players" pretended they were the Miami Dolphins.

The players' strike resulted from football's meteoric growth in the 1970s. Television networks were setting all-time rating highs showing NFL games. Advertising revenues multiplied two to three times. With the influx of money, football franchises became valuable commodities. Longtime family ownership began to disappear, replaced by new millionaires and billionaires who saw the NFL as a business and a sports team as an investment.

Like many business owners, the NFL's team owners hated competition. They knew a bidding war for players would simply raise salaries and reduce profits. Since 1961, the NFL teams had practiced revenue sharing. This meant they split the network television money equally. Revenue sharing allowed NFL franchises to exist in markets as large as New York City and as small as Green Bay, Wisconsin, because national broadcast rights provided all teams with an equal economic foundation. (The national television deals are still by far the greatest source of income for NFL teams; each team received almost $100 million in 2007.) However, revenue sharing meant there was little economic incentive for one team to try to outbid another team for players. Because all teams received the same share, there was not much point in spending millions of dollars on players.

For this reason, the NFL players thought they were being exploited. The average playing career in the NFL was (and is) incredibly short—less than four years. While some exceptional

In 1987, NFL players went on strike in support of free agency and higher salaries. Here, Dan Marino walks the picket line outside Joe Robbie Stadium before replacement players suited up for the Dolphins in their October 11 game against the Kansas City Chiefs. Although some NFL players crossed the picket line, the majority refused to play during the first three weeks of October that season.

players such as Dan Marino have long careers, most players leave the game after a few years due to injury or being cut by a team. In addition, while the NFL publicized multimillion-dollar contracts such as Marino's, it did not highlight the fact that many lesser players made substantially smaller amounts of money.

For example, Jimmy Cefalo was an outstanding Dolphins receiver who caught a touchdown pass in Super Bowl XVII. He also caught the Marino pass that broke the record for most touchdown passes in a season. Yet Cefalo retired after only six seasons in the NFL. He said,

> There was no future for me in football, especially at that time when they weren't paying a lot of money. The salaries weren't always what they are today . . . my first year salary was $35,000. I left football to make more money and to provide for my family. Catching another hundred balls would have been okay, but not very important.

If the NFL was making billions of dollars in the 1980s, the players felt they deserved a larger share of the pie. In 1982, the NFL season was reduced from a 16-game schedule to 9 games as a result of a 57-day players strike. During this time, no NFL games were played at all. The strike was finally settled by a compromise agreement that was scheduled to run through the 1986 season. This agreement gave the players a percentage of the NFL's gross revenue. It also established certain minimum salaries for players based on their years of experience. Many NFL players were still dissatisfied. They wanted true free agency so they could sell their services to the highest bidder.

NFL players had almost no choice as to where they would play. However, between 1983 and 1985, a rival to the NFL existed in the USFL. The USFL signed top-notch talent such as Heisman Trophy winners Mike Rozier and Herschel Walker, as well as Doug Flutie, Reggie White, Jim Kelly, Steve Young,

Craig James, and Brian Sipe. Competition with the USFL meant NFL salaries started to rise—from an average of $90,000 in 1982 to $230,000 in 1987. However, when the USFL folded in 1985, the NFL again faced no competition.

The market for professional football in the United States had not yet hit the saturation point. Super Bowl XIX, in which Joe Montana's 49ers defeated Dan Marino's Dolphins, was viewed on television by 116 million people, more than any other live event up to that time. In 1985, the Chicago-Miami Monday Night Football game had the highest rating of any prime-time game in NFL history. More than 25 million people watched Miami's victory in that game.

When the labor contract came to an end in 1987, the players, through the NFL Players Association, asked for true free agency, as well as 55 percent of the gross revenues. (In 2007, they received about 65 percent.) Because the USFL had folded in 1985, the owners once again had their monopoly intact and saw no reason to negotiate. The players decided to go on strike after the second week of the season.

However, the situation differed from 1982. In that strike, the networks paid the owners in advance for television rights. In 1987, the only way the owners could receive television money was to make sure games were played. So although games scheduled for the third weekend were canceled, games of weeks four, five, and six were played with replacement players, mostly those who had been cut in preseason. A few veterans also crossed the picket line, such as Joe Montana, Giants linebacker Lawrence Taylor, Cowboys running back Tony Dorsett, Raiders defensive end Howie Long, and Cowboys quarterback Danny White. The television networks aired these games as if the hastily assembled teams were actually the same quality as regular NFL teams.

Faced with wavering support from its members and the willingness of the networks to broadcast the bogus games, the union voted to go back to work after 24 days. The same day, however, the players filed an antitrust lawsuit against the NFL claiming that the league was an illegal monopoly.

That is why Dan Marino found himself walking a picket line in 1987 and his consecutive-game starting streak was never officially recognized. Marino later said, "There's one number that's not in the record books—and never officially will be—that I might be most proud about: starting 145 consecutive games. That's by my count, at least . . . the two [sic] scab games played during the 1987 players' strike officially interrupted the streak according to the NFL gatekeepers. I sure didn't play in those." (The streak has since been broken by Green Bay's incredible quarterback Brett Favre, who started 253 consecutive regular-season games through the 2007 season.)

COMING BACK AFTER THE STRIKE

Marino was happy to return to the Dolphins after the strike. He threw for 303 yards and four touchdowns against the Buffalo Bills in a 34-31 loss, which dropped Miami to 2–4. But the Dolphins won five out of their next seven games, and in Week 15, they were 7–6 and needed a win against the Washington Redskins to keep their playoff hopes alive. With about a minute to go, Marino threw a six-yard touchdown pass to Mark Duper to give the Dolphins a crucial 23-21 win. After the game, Washington All-Pro defensive lineman Dexter Manley said, "He's his own pass protector. All you need is him and the center. He can take it from there. . . . I think Joe Montana is a great quarterback, but Dan Marino is the best."

Marino led the AFC in touchdown passes (26), completions (263), and was second in passing yardage (3,245) that year. However, the Dolphins lost their final game of the season to the Patriots, 24-10, and only finished 8–7 (7–5 in nonstrike games) in the strike-shortened year. Unfortunately, the Dolphins did not make the playoffs for the second year in a row. The Redskins team that Marino and the Dolphins beat in the last seconds went on to win Super Bowl XXII. The

Dan Marino changes the play at the line of scrimmage during the Dolphins' 20-14 win over the Cincinnati Bengals on November 8, 1987. Although Marino did not play in four games due to the strike that year, he still led the AFC in touchdown passes (26) and finished second in passing yards (3,245) to Bengals quarterback Boomer Esiason.

Washington players had been instructed by their head coach, Joe Gibbs, to remain united throughout the strike; not one of the regular Redskins players crossed the picket line during the period of scab games. This went a long way in helping them win the Super Bowl.

The next season, 1988, Miami started strong but collapsed at the end of the season. The team lost six of its last seven games and had its first losing season (6–10) since 1976. Nonetheless, Marino had another solid season statistically. He became the first quarterback in NFL history to pass for more than 4,000 yards four times in a career. He also threw his 193rd career touchdown pass, setting a new Dolphins record. It had taken Bob Griese 14 seasons to set that record; Marino had broken it in six.

Not surprisingly, Marino's most amazing performance that year was against the New York Jets. On October 23, Marino completed 35 of 60 passes and threw for a career-high 521 yards. He became one of only a handful of quarterbacks in NFL history to throw for more than 500 yards in a game.

THE NFL'S 500-YARD CLUB
(THROUGH THE 2007 SEASON)

RANK	YARDS	QUARTERBACK	TEAM	YEAR
1	554	Norm Van Brocklin	Los Angeles Rams	1951
2	527	Warren Moon	Houston Oilers	1990
3	522	Boomer Esiason	Arizona Cardinals	1996
4	521	Dan Marino	Miami Dolphins	1988
5	513	Phil Simms	New York Giants	1985
6	510	Drew Brees	New Orleans Saints	2006
7	509	Vince Ferragamo	Los Angeles Rams	1982
8	505	Y. A. Tittle	New York Giants	1962

However, Marino also threw five interceptions; three of them to rookie Jets cornerback Erik McMillan. The Jets led the entire game and won, 44-30.

The Dolphins struggled again in 1989. In Marino's seventh season in professional football, the Dolphins finished 8–8 and missed the playoffs for the fourth straight year. The playoff appearances of Marino's first three years were now just a distant memory. In the last game of the season, the Dolphins could have won the AFC East Division by beating the Kansas City Chiefs. Marino hit Mark Clayton to tie the score with four minutes to play, but the Chiefs kicked a field goal in the last minute to beat the Dolphins, 27-24, and keep them out of the playoffs. Marino could barely contain his frustration: "I don't like to talk all the time about being frustrated. If you talk about it enough, sooner or later, you believe it."

ENDING FOUR YEARS OF FRUSTRATION

After four years of futility, Marino and the Dolphins righted the ship in 1990. The Dolphins finally put together a decent defense and finished with a 12–4 record, second in the AFC East Division to the Buffalo Bills. The offense did not depend as much on Marino's arm, and he threw only 21 touchdown passes all season. In the wild-card round of the playoffs, the Dolphins hosted the Kansas City Chiefs. The Chiefs built a 16-3 lead, but Marino had a spectacular fourth quarter, completing all eight of his passes for 101 yards and two touchdowns. The winning score came with 2:28 left to play when Marino's 12-yard touchdown pass to Mark Clayton capped an 85-yard drive. The Dolphins beat the Chiefs, 17-16. Marino was ecstatic: "This showed a lot," he said after the game, "because a lot of guys showed a lot of guts, a lot of courage."

The win against Kansas City set up a divisional showdown with the Bills in Buffalo. At the time of the kickoff, snow was falling heavily. Usually teams try to run the ball when the weather is bad, but not the Dolphins or the Bills. The game turned into a shootout between the two 1983 first-round draft choices. The Bills jumped out to a 13-3 lead in the first quarter and the two teams matched each other score for score for the rest of the game. Marino threw for 323 yards, three touchdowns, and two interceptions. Duper caught three passes for 113 yards, including a 64-yard touchdown. Kelly threw for three touchdowns and 339 yards. In the end, the Bills won, 44-34. After the game, Don Shula looked back on the season. "When you think about numbers, 1984 was mind-boggling. But even though [Marino's] numbers didn't reflect it, I thought he had his best year last year with his leadership on the field and in the locker room."

In August 1991, Marino signed what was then the most lucrative contract in NFL history: $25 million for five years. Dolphins president Tim Robbie said, "We feel Dan is one of the best players in the history of the NFL and the contract reflects that. As long as we have No. 13 on the field, we have a shot at the Super Bowl." The contract not only reflected Marino's value, but also the incredible growth of professional football in the United States. Marino's first contract in 1983 had paid him $2 million for four years. After his first few seasons, Marino signed a six-year, $9 million deal. Now he was the highest-paid player in the league.

However, halfway through the 1991 season, the Dolphins were only 3–5. For the first time, there was some unhappiness with Marino in Miami. Some fans began to feel that Marino should have been winning a lot more games for the money he was making. After all, $25 million could pay for a lot of linebackers. Marino admitted, "We're not getting open like we should, and we're not blocking like we should. We're just not making big plays. But you know, I'm the quarterback and to a certain extent I should control that."

However, after their poor start, the Dolphins came back and won five of their next six games. They were 8–6 with two games left. Then they lost to San Diego, 38-30, setting up a classic game in the final week of the season with—who else—the New York Jets.

The importance of the game could not be understated: The winner would clinch the final AFC **wild-card** spot in the playoffs; the loser's season would end. The game was hard-fought,

STABILITY IN THE NFL

Since the 1987 strike, the NFL has enjoyed labor harmony between the players and the owners. This is especially impressive considering other American sports have had major problems. Baseball's World Series was cancelled in 1994 because of a players strike, the NBA season was almost entirely wiped out by a 202-day lockout in 1998–1999, and the entire 2004–2005 NHL season was cancelled because the owners locked out the players.

The key to football's successful labor-management relations came from the lawsuit the players filed at the end of the 1987 strike seeking free agency for themselves. The lawsuit slowly worked its way up through the courts before it was settled in 1992. As a result of the settlement, the NFL and the NFL Players Association compromised on free agency and a **salary cap.** This agreement ended years of labor unrest in football. The resulting 1993 collective bargaining agreement has been quietly extended five times since then. The agreement permitted free agency in return for salary caps tied to a formula based on the players' share of total league revenues. Although tricky issues such as who gets the money for stadium naming rights, luxury boxes, and team merchandising have threatened to cause problems, the agreement was extended once again in March 2006 to last through the 2011 season.

and the score seesawed back and forth. The Jets were ahead 17-13 with just 3:42 left in the game. Then Marino led one of his famous fourth-quarter comebacks. He drove the Dolphins 70 yards downfield. Faced with a fourth-and-1 on the 1-yard line, Marino hit tight end Ferrell Edmunds for a touchdown to give the Dolphins the lead, 20-17, with just 44 seconds remaining. However, when the Jets got the ball back, they drove down the field in less than a minute and tied the game on a 44-yard field goal. The Jets eventually won the game in overtime with a 30-yard field goal, ending the Dolphins' season in disappointing fashion.

Coach Shula was despondent after the game. "We had control of it in San Diego and couldn't do the job," he said, "and then we had control again here and couldn't do the job. This [loss] will last a long time, for me and for us." Marino was equally upset. "The way we played, we don't deserve to be in the playoffs," he said.

Although the names around Marino had changed, the seasons began to blend together with distressing similarity. The Dolphins won their first six games in 1992 behind the running of Mark Higgs. Marino's new favorite target was tight end Keith Jackson, newly acquired from the Philadelphia Eagles as a free agent. However, the team again began to slip in the second half of the season, splitting its last 10 games to finish 11–5. This was still good enough to win the AFC East Division and earn the second seed in the playoffs.

In the divisional round of the playoffs, the Dolphins destroyed the San Diego Chargers, 31-0. The Miami defense held San Diego quarterback Stan Humphries to just 18 of 44 passing for 140 yards and intercepted him four times. Marino threw three touchdown passes in the second quarter for the easy win.

Unfortunately for Marino, the story was reversed in the AFC Championship Game. The Buffalo Bills, who had upset top-seeded Pittsburgh in the divisional round, intercepted Marino two times, recovered three fumbles (one by Marino), forced four sacks, and held Miami to just 33 rushing yards. Buffalo kicker Steve Christie recorded an NFL-playoff-record-tying five field goals as the Dolphins were defeated, 29-10. Marino did not know it at the time, but he had just made his final appearance in an AFC Championship Game. He would go no further than the divisional round of the playoffs through the remaining seven years of his career.

The following year, Miami was favored at the start of the season to make it back to the AFC Championship Game. However, the 1993 season would not be at all like other Dolphins seasons. Marino had been extremely durable up to that year. He had been a professional quarterback for 10 years and never suffered a major injury. He had started an astonishing 145 consecutive nonstrike games. He had endured five operations on his right knee during the streak, but he never missed a game. Within a few weeks in 1989, Marino broke a rib, hurt his elbow, and then hurt his shoulder. He did not practice for a month, but he did not miss a start. It seemed as if he were almost superhuman.

OVERCOMING INJURY

However, after starting 3–1 in 1993, time finally caught up to him in a game against the Cleveland Browns. After throwing a swing pass, Marino, who was untouched on the play, crumpled to the ground in pain. He could not get up on his own. He had ruptured his right Achilles tendon—the tendon that joins the calf muscle to the heel bone. Marino would say later, "I felt like I'd been shot." Tearing an Achilles tendon is a very serious injury that forces many athletes to retire. "Sometimes you do take it for granted," Marino said. "You go out there and play every Sunday, and nothing happens. Then all of a sudden, when something does, it's a shock."

Marino was out of the lineup for the rest of the season, ending the longest consecutive-game starting streak by a quarterback since the 1970 merger. (Due to the games Marino

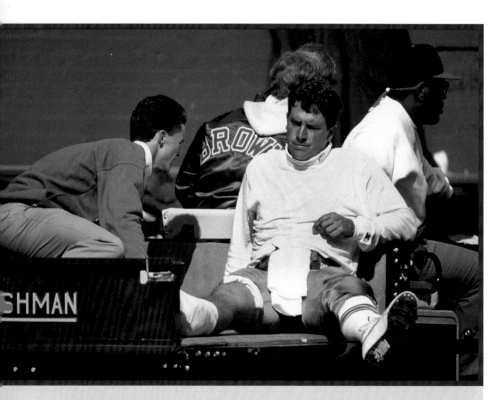

Many football prognosticators thought that Dan Marino and the Miami Dolphins might finally return to the Super Bowl in 1993. However, after a 3–1 start, Marino tore his Achilles tendon during Miami's game with the Cleveland Browns on October 10 and missed the remainder of the season. Here, Marino is carted off the field at Cleveland Municipal Stadium after the injury.

missed during the 1987 strike, Ron Jaworski officially owned the longest consecutive-starts streak by a quarterback at 116 games.) Months of grueling rehabilitation followed. After surgery, the tendon still was not healing properly. Marino could not rise up on his toes. That meant it would be very difficult to strengthen his calf. Many Miami fans wondered if the 32-year-old quarterback would ever be able to play again. He had already had several knee operations, his mobility was decreasing, and he was not getting any younger. In Marino's absence, backup quarterback Scott Mitchell played extremely well until he also was injured. After starting the season 9–2, Miami lost its last five games and missed the playoffs.

For the first time in a decade, Miami had a quarterback controversy. Many members of the media and some fans wanted to keep the younger Mitchell (who was a free agent after the season) rather than the aging Marino. In the end, Miami decided to stick with Marino. Mitchell signed a free-agent contract with the Detroit Lions and went on to have a solid career. As insurance, the Dolphins signed ex-University of Miami quarterback Bernie Kosar.

Wearing a protective brace on his ankle and with a right calf that was visibly weakened, Marino was once again Miami's starting quarterback at the start of the 1994 season. Many people feared the injury would affect his passing motion or his ability to plant his feet. In preseason, Marino seemed to struggle to find his rhythm. The forebodings increased. In the final exhibition game, he only completed 4 of 12 passes for 37 yards. He also threw two interceptions, one of which was returned for a touchdown.

The season opener was a home game versus the New England Patriots. Would Marino be able to come back? Even he had his doubts. Leading up to the game, it had rained heavily and the baseball infield was very muddy. (Since the 1993 season, the Dolphins had shared Joe Robbie Stadium with Major League Baseball's Florida Marlins.) The Patriots led 14-10 at halftime, but in the second half both quarterbacks started bombing away. Despite the conditions, Marino and Drew Bledsoe put up an astonishing combined 894 yards and nine touchdowns through the air. At the end of the day, Marino had completed 23 of 42 passes for 473 yards and five touchdowns. Marino clearly remembered the last touchdown:

Fourth down. Ball at the Patriots' 39. Three minutes to go. We trailed by three points and needed 5 yards for a first down. The called play was a short pass for a first down.

But coming to the line I noticed Irving Fryar had the kind of one-on-one bump-and-run coverage that through the years I always took a shot on. Duper. Clayton. Fryar. Just make some eye contact to set the play at the line and go long. But would I do it this first game back with the day on the line? Was there any doubt? After the touchdown, after we celebrated, after the 39-35 win, even Patriots coach Bill Parcels walked over, shook my hand, and said, "Not bad for a guy on one ankle."

So it turned out that Marino was far from finished. In fact, he led the Dolphins to a 10–6 record and yet another AFC East Division title. He finished the season with a team-record 385 completions. He broke his own NFL record, throwing for more than 4,000 yards for the sixth time in his career. For his efforts, the NFL named him Comeback Player of the Year.

He also participated in yet another classic game against the Jets at the Meadowlands. On November 27, the Jets trailed the Dolphins by one game for the AFC East Division lead. With first place on the line, the Jets held a 24-6 lead after three quarters. However, Marino led the Dolphins back with two touchdowns to make the score 24-21. Then Marino got the ball one last time and drove the Dolphins down the field to the Jets' 8-yard line with 30 seconds remaining. The Dolphins had no more timeouts and the clock was winding down. Marino sprinted to the line of scrimmage and yelled, "Clock! Clock! Clock!" Marino took the snap from center and motioned as if he was going to spike the ball to stop the clock. On the snap, the entire Jets defense relaxed because they assumed Marino would spike the ball. Instead, he fired a pass to the corner of the end zone into the hands of Mark Ingram, his fourth touchdown catch of the game. The touchdown gave the Dolphins a 28-24 victory, and Miami went on to win the division. The Jets fell apart after that play and lost all of their remaining games. In football legend, the game is often known as the "Clock Play" game.

Unfortunately, once again, the season ended dismally. Miami started well by beating the Kansas City Chiefs in the wild-card round of the playoffs. Both teams scored on each of their first three possessions of the game, and the score was tied 17-17 at halftime. Joe Montana, now Kansas City's quarterback, was playing in his last NFL game before retiring and threw two touchdowns in the first half. However, Marino's Dolphins took the opening kickoff of the second half and marched 64 yards, capped by Marino's seven-yard touchdown pass to wide receiver Irving Fryar. The Dolphins forced two turnovers in the second half, and Miami won, 27-17.

In the divisional round of the playoffs, Miami lost a heartbreaker to the San Diego Chargers, 22-21. Marino threw three touchdowns in the first half: two to tight end Keith Jackson for eight and nine yards, and a 16-yarder to wide receiver Mike Williams. However, the Chargers rallied from a 21-6 halftime deficit by limiting the Dolphins' offense to only 16 plays in the second half. The Dolphins only ran the ball eight times in the entire game, choosing to live or die by Marino's arm. The Chargers later took the lead, 22-21, with 35 seconds left. Miami kicker Pete Stoyanovich had a chance to kick a game-winning 48-yard field goal on the final play of the game, but it sailed wide. Once again, Marino had come up short in his bid to return to the Super Bowl. He said, "I had [three] touchdown passes in that game, but the thing that sticks out was what I could have done differently at the end. We had 32 seconds. We moved the ball. Then I had two downs to put Pete at least ten yards closer. And I threw two incompletions."

Marino had now been with the Dolphins for 12 seasons. Despite all the records, highlights, and playoff appearances, they had only appeared in one Super Bowl during those 12 years. Marino said, "I don't want to walk away from the game without getting to another Super Bowl, but I love playing and I can feel good about my career."

A New Era

Coach Don Shula had led the Miami Dolphins to two Super Bowl victories and the first undefeated season in modern NFL history. He held the NFL record for most career wins with 347 and was one of the most well-respected coaches of all time. Nonetheless, Miami's failure to win another Super Bowl in the 1980s and 1990s upset some fans and members of the local media. They began to imply that "the game had passed Shula by."

A change in the team's ownership did not help Shula's position. Joe Robbie was the original owner of the Dolphins and ran the team until his death in 1990. When Robbie died, his family found it difficult to run the team. Wayne Huizenga, a billionaire who made his money with Waste Management and Blockbuster Video, purchased half of the Dolphins and their stadium in 1990. Three years later, Huizenga bought out the remaining shares of the Dolphins to become full owner. Huizenga, like many corporate-heads-turned-sports-team-owners, wanted the greater public stage that owning a football team provided.

THE GREATEST QUARTERBACK OF ALL TIME?

In 1995, many people picked the Dolphins to win the AFC Championship. During the off-season, the Dolphins had signed many talented and expensive free agents and acquired defensive help in trades. That season, Marino broke the NFL career records formerly held by Fran Tarkenton for passing yards, touchdown passes, and completions. When Marino broke Tarkenton's record for most completions in NFL history, the former Minnesota Vikings quarterback sent Marino a message that appeared on the Miami scoreboard: "You are one of the greatest quarterbacks who has ever played. You've earned it. I'm honored that you're the one who's breaking [the record]."

Marino's old idol, Pittsburgh Steelers great Terry Bradshaw, was equally impressed. "He is just an exceptional quarterback," Bradshaw said. "Throwing for that many yards is mind-boggling, especially when you consider that since his rookie year he has been a marked man. [Opponents] were saying, 'We have to stop this passing attack,' and they've done everything in the world they can, and they can't, and they won't, and they never will. . . . He is the greatest quarterback that ever played the game."

However, the Dolphins as a team had a disappointing season. They won their first four games and then lost six of the next eight. They finished with a 9–7 record, good enough for only second place in the AFC East Division. Then the Dolphins were blown out, 37-22, in the wild-card round of the playoffs by the Buffalo Bills. In that game, Marino threw a career-high 64 passes, completing 33 for an astonishing 422 yards. Unfortunately, many of the completions came in the fourth quarter when the Bills already led, 27-0. The number that

During the 1995 season, Dan Marino broke three of Fran Tarkenton's NFL career records—passing yards (47,003), touchdown passes (342), and completions (3,686). Here, Tarkenton congratulates Marino before the Dolphins' Monday Night Football game against Kansas City on December 11 of that year.

caught people's attention was Buffalo's 341 rushing yards—an NFL playoff record. Once again, the Dolphins' defense had not shown up when it mattered the most. It would be the third time that the Bills and quarterback Jim Kelly knocked Marino out of the playoffs between 1990 and 1995.

The loss meant the end of an era in Miami. The press and local radio talk-show hosts urged Huizenga to replace Shula. All of Shula's good years counted for little against the frustration of the team's supporters. Shula recognized the pressure and stepped down as head coach of the Dolphins at the end of the season. He left with the NFL records for regular-season wins (328), total victories (347), most games coached (526), and most Super Bowl appearances (6). Shula's teams almost always were among the least penalized in the NFL. He and Marino had won 123 games together. But they had not won a Super Bowl together.

A NEW HEAD COACH

The Miami Dolphins knew they would need a big-name coach to replace Shula. They could not just hire an up-and-coming assistant coach. They wanted a coach who would not be intimidated by Shula's long shadow. They decided to hire Jimmy Johnson.

When Johnson replaced Shula, he had already won an NCAA title as coach of the University of Miami in 1987. In 1989, he left Florida to take over as head coach of the Dallas Cowboys in the NFL. College coaches often have a difficult time making the transition to professional football. In Johnson's first season with the Cowboys, they won one game and lost 15. Many people said, "I told you so." However, by his third season, the Cowboys had made the playoffs. In his fourth season, they won the Super Bowl. Then he won another Super Bowl before resigning as head coach after the 1993 season. From 1994 to 1996, Johnson had been serving as a television analyst. On accepting the offer to coach the Dolphins, he said, "I came here to do one thing: win another [Super Bowl]. And on the clock in my head, I'm looking at three years."

Johnson had the reputation of being a defensive specialist. Marino was not getting any younger, and the team could not always put up 30 or more points in a game, especially in the playoffs. Marino liked the challenge of working with a new coach. In an early meeting with Johnson, Marino said that he did not care if he threw only 10 passes a game. All he wanted to do was "win games and have a chance to win the championship. That's what makes me happy." This went along with Johnson's way of thinking. Johnson said, "I want to have a football team that's able to go out on the field and win a game offensively and defensively."

The Dolphins opened the Jimmy Johnson era in 1996 by beating the New England Patriots, 24-10. Rookie running back Karim Abdul-Jabbar ran for 115 yards, and Marino only threw for 176 yards. "I don't want to ride Dan Marino in every football game," said Johnson after the game. "I want the team to win."

The new-look Dolphins won their first three games of the season, but then Marino got hurt. He suffered a hairline fracture of the ankle in a 10-6 loss to the Indianapolis Colts and missed the next three games. When he returned against the Dallas Cowboys, he played poorly and the Dolphins lost, 29-10. The season began to slip away again.

In December, the Dolphins had a do-or-die game at home against the New York Giants. Johnson was so confident the Dolphins would win that he predicted, "Everybody is going to have smiles on their faces after Sunday. You can count on it." Only it did not work out that way. The Giants continuously blitzed, and Marino could not avoid the rush as he had when he was younger. He was sacked three times and intercepted twice as the Giants beat the Dolphins, 17-7. After the game, Giants cornerback Jason Sehorn gave an honest, if sad, evaluation of Marino:

> I'm glad I caught him [Marino] now in year thirteen [of his career], because can you imagine how good he was years ago when he could move? I mean, I've never seen a guy play with so many braces. It looked like he had braces up to his waist. He just has no mobility and we wanted to force him to move around the pocket. I still have a great deal of respect for him, but he's just not the same guy.

In the end, the Dolphins only went 8–8 in 1996 under Jimmy Johnson, compared to 9–7 in Don Shula's last season. While Abdul-Jabbar rushed for 1,116 yards, the Dolphins still failed to make the playoffs. Marino had thrown his 4,000th completion and exceeded 50,000 passing yards for his career. However, the records did not mean quite as much anymore. He said, "It's pretty tough to take right now because another year's work is down the drain. We've been working hard and the bad part is it didn't work out the way we wanted it to." Now in the twilight of his career, Marino was playing on creaky knees, a bad ankle, and nerve root irritation in his neck that weakened his arms and legs. Yet from each injury, Marino returned with more determination to capture a Super Bowl title. He sensed that his legacy as a quarterback would be determined by what his team did or failed to do.

The disappointment of not making the playoffs in 1996 did not dent Jimmy Johnson's confidence. After his first season as Dolphins coach, he declared, "We let some things slip through our fingers this year. That won't happen again next year." However, the next year, tension began to develop between Johnson and Marino. Marino struggled in the season opener against the Indianapolis Colts before the Dolphins finally won, 16-10. After the game, Johnson admitted that he considered benching Marino. In the months that followed, Johnson seemed reluctant to praise Marino; instead, he singled out his mistakes. Yet after a 33-30 win against the Detroit Lions in December, the Dolphins were 9–5 and had an excellent chance to win the AFC East Division. However, in the next-to-last game of the regular season against the Colts, Marino fumbled twice and had his second-lowest passing yardage game (71 yards) in his NFL career. He watched most of the second half from the bench as the Colts embarrassed the Dolphins, 41-0.

The Dolphins then concluded their season with a disappointing home loss, 14-12, to the New England Patriots. The game cost them the AFC East Division title, and instead of playing at home in the wild-card round of the playoffs, they had to travel to New England for a rematch. It would be one of the worst games of Marino's career. The Dolphins' offense gained a paltry 162 yards, and Marino only completed 17 of 43 passes for

141 yards and two interceptions. New England won easily, 17-3, and another Dolphins season had ended in frustration.

Johnson began to wonder if he could win a title with Marino. The quarterback would be entering his sixteenth professional season in 1998. He had tons of experience but no mobility. Yet when Johnson threatened to bench Marino, the public backlash was overwhelming. Both men were successful, driven, and competitive. Neither was entirely comfortable with someone with an ego and public following as large as his own. Marino especially did not like it when Johnson blamed him for the team's lack of success during Johnson's private conversations with the media.

Johnson had been given complete control over personnel decisions and was expected to put together a championship defense. The Dolphins did draft several excellent defensive players who would eventually make the Pro Bowl. However, several high-profile first-round busts tarnished the coach's draft record. Johnson had promised a Super Bowl in three years. The third year had arrived.

In 1998, the Dolphins went 10–6. This would be their best record in the Jimmy Johnson era. They were one of only two teams to defeat the Denver Broncos in the regular season. A young defense allowed an NFL-low 265 points. Miami finished second in the AFC East Division (behind the Jets) and drew their nemesis, the Buffalo Bills, in the wild-card game. However, Johnson's defense forced five Bills turnovers, including a fumble by Buffalo quarterback Doug Flutie at the Miami 5-yard line with 17 seconds left in the game. Miami finally beat the Bills in the playoffs, 24-17.

However, the Dolphins were annihilated in the divisional round of the playoffs by the Denver Broncos, 38-3. Denver outgained Miami in rushing yards, 250–14, and scored touchdowns on its first three possessions. Marino, in his only playoff matchup with quarterback John Elway, threw for 243 yards, but also was intercepted twice. Miami did not score a

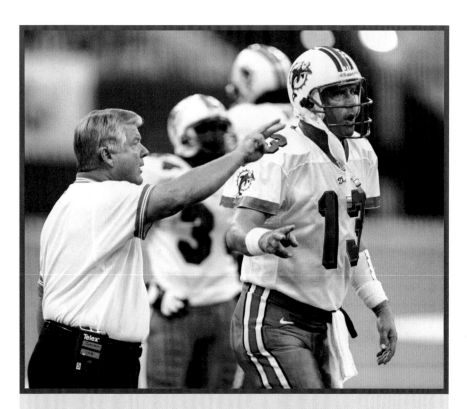

Dolphins head coach Jimmy Johnson, who replaced Don Shula after the 1995 season, had a tumultuous relationship with Dan Marino. Although Dolphins fans hoped Johnson would lead them back to the Super Bowl, he was only able to guide them to two wild-card playoff wins and a 36–28 regular-season record in his four years as head coach.

single touchdown, and Denver went on to win the Super Bowl in Elway's last season.

Jimmy Johnson's three years had come and gone. The Dolphins had not won the Super Bowl, but they had made some progress every year under Johnson. So it was a surprise when Johnson temporarily resigned as Dolphins head coach in January 1999. He claimed he was too burned out to continue. Ironically, Johnson seems to have reversed his decision after Marino pleaded with him to return. The Dolphins brought in Dave Wannstedt, a former assistant under Johnson at both the University of Miami and in Dallas, as defensive coordinator to ease the burden on Johnson. Johnson decided to give it one more shot. He told the team's supporters, "We've got a shot. We've got a chance to be special. There's not many teams that have a chance to do this. That's why I came back."

THE BEGINNING OF THE END

The Super Bowl–level expectations ended up putting too much pressure on the team. Miami started the season 8–2 but then lost five of its last six games to finish 9–7. Marino was now more injury-prone and less consistent than he had ever been during his career. As the team faded, Johnson's relationship with Marino dissolved completely. The head coach publicly criticized his star quarterback for poor decisions and costly turnovers. He began using Damon Huard, Marino's backup, more and more. Marino missed five games and most of a sixth because of a neck injury. One of Marino's lowest points during the 1999 season came in the Dolphins' Thanksgiving game versus the Cowboys. In his first game back after missing a month due to injury, Marino threw five interceptions in the Dolphins' 20-0 loss. Huard finished the season completing 125 of 216 passes (to Marino's 204 of 369) with a higher **passer rating** than Marino. In fact, Huard was 5–1 in games he started.

However, the season would not be complete without at least one entertaining game against the New York Jets. The contest on December 27, 1999, Marino's last against the Jets, certainly lived up to expectations. The Jets' quarterback, a young backup named Ray Lucas, completed 11 of 23 passes for 190 yards and three touchdowns. But Marino put on one of his last great performances. He completed 29 of 52 passes for 322 yards and three touchdowns (and three interceptions). It would be the last of Marino's NFL regular-season record of 63 career games with 300 yards passing, but the Jets came away with a 38-31 victory.

Yet despite the Dolphins' collapse at the end of the season, it was Marino who helped the team rally in the second half of

DAN MARINO IN THE PLAYOFFS

YEAR	RECORD	FINISH	PLAYOFFS
1983	12–4	1st AFC East	Lost in divisional round to Seattle Seahawks, 27-20
1984	14–2	1st AFC East	Won in divisional round against Seattle Seahawks, 31-10
			Won AFC Championship against Pittsburgh Steelers, 45-28
			Lost Super Bowl XIX to San Francisco 49ers, 38-16
1985	12–4	1st AFC East	Won in divisional round against Cleveland Browns, 24-21
			Lost AFC Championship to New England Patriots, 31-14
1986	8–8	3rd AFC East	———
1987	8–7	3rd AFC East	———
1988	6–10	5th AFC East	———
1989	8–8	3rd AFC East	———
1990	12–4	2nd AFC East	Won in wild-card round against Kansas City Chiefs, 17-16
			Lost in divisional round to Buffalo Bills, 44-34
1991	8–8	3rd AFC East	———
1992	11–5	1st AFC East	Won in divisional round against San Diego Chargers, 31-0
			Lost AFC Championship to Buffalo Bills, 29-10
1993	9–7	2nd AFC East	———
1994	10–6	1st AFC East	Won in wild-card round against Kansas City Chiefs, 27-17
			Lost in divisional round to San Diego Chargers, 22-21
1995	9–7	3rd AFC East	Lost in wild-card round to Buffalo Bills, 37-22
1996	8–8	4th AFC East	———
1997	9–7	2nd AFC East	Lost in wild-card round to New England Patriots, 17-3
1998	10–6	2nd AFC East	Won in wild-card round against Buffalo Bills, 24-17
			Lost in divisional round to Denver Broncos, 38-3
1999	9–7	3rd AFC East	Won in wild-card round against Seattle, Seahawks, 20-17
			Lost in divisional round to Jacksonville Jaguars, 62-7

the wild-card game at Seattle against the Seahawks. Marino threw for 196 yards and a touchdown, leading his team to its first playoff win on the road since Miami defeated the Pittsburgh Steelers in the 1972 AFC Championship Game at Three Rivers Stadium. That meant it was the first playoff road win of Marino's career. It also was his thirty-seventh comeback win. Marino had played well enough in the 20-17 victory against the Seahawks that fans and players thought that this might be the Dolphins' year.

However, Johnson and Marino's final bid to win a Super Bowl together ended with a disastrous 62-7 playoff loss at Jacksonville. It was the worst defeat in Dolphins history. The Jaguars shredded Jimmy Johnson's defense, accumulating 520 total offensive yards. The Jaguars' defense forced seven turnovers and held the Dolphins to 131 total yards. At one point in the second quarter, Marino was 3 of 11 for 12 yards, and the Dolphins trailed, 41-0. Huard replaced Marino in the second half, an ignominious end to a spectacular career. It was the most lopsided postseason contest since the Chicago Bears defeated the Washington Redskins, 73-0, in the 1940 NFL Championship Game.

Johnson was finished. The coach retired the next day, replaced by Dave Wannstedt. As Marino noted in his autobiography, "There would have been better ways to go out than a 62-7 loss in Jacksonville. Heck, any way might have been better, including on a shield. That one sat like a stone in your stomach, but that's how it goes. . . . You don't get to write your own script. You just take the games as they come."

Jimmy Johnson did not live up to expectations. In fact, he did not even match Don Shula's record. Johnson did not even come close to winning a Super Bowl in Miami. In four years, he had led the team to a 36–28 regular-season record. Johnson's overall winning percentage at Miami was 56 percent versus 66 percent for Don Shula. In fairness to Johnson, the

Dan Marino fights back his emotions as he announces to the media on March 13, 2000, that he plans to retire after 17 seasons with the Dolphins. For Marino, the decision to retire was difficult, but in the end, he felt that his body could not withstand another year of punishment.

Dolphins posted a regular-season record of 41–23 from 2000 to 2003 with a core group of players assembled by Johnson and his staff.

When asked about his four-year association with Johnson, Marino said: "I would just have to say that our relationship was up and down at times . . . we had some great, great days together and some fun times and sometimes I wasn't very happy here while he was coaching and that is just being honest."

In February 2000, Marino exercised a clause in his contract and became a free agent. Would he play an eighteenth season? When the Dolphins signed free-agent quarterback Jay Fiedler to a three-year, $3.8 million contract, it was clear that Marino had played his last game in Miami. Marino briefly considered offers to play one more year for the Pittsburgh Steelers or the Minnesota Vikings. He said,

> Any time you play football . . . you get excited when a coach calls you. . . . And to be honest with you, they have some outstanding receivers, guys that I would have loved to throw to. I was excited about it. But the emotional swings that I had back and forth in those weeks or so that we had meetings and we discussed my possibility of going to the Vikings was incredible. I considered it seriously.

In the end, Marino reluctantly decided to turn down the offer. He felt his body just could not take the pounding of another season.

And so, on March 13, 2000, Dan Marino retired after 17 seasons as quarterback of the Miami Dolphins. "I'm going to miss it," Marino said, struggling to fight back tears at a news conference. "I'm going to miss everything about it. . . . Most of all I am going to miss Sunday afternoons." Marino's wife, children, parents, and former coach Don Shula were all with him in the team meeting room. Claire, Marino's wife, cried during much of the news conference. Jimmy Johnson did not attend.

After the Cheering Stopped

When Dan Marino retired at age 38, he had played football every year since the fourth grade. Throwing a ball had defined him as a person and given him a purpose in life. Now the time had come to let it go. That would not be easy. When asked what he missed about playing, he responded, "What *don't* I? The guys. The games. The tingly feeling of strutting into an opponent's stadium on a big day, with all their fans screaming—like you're on a mission. . . . I even miss the practices." Yet even as a player, Marino knew football was only half of life. He said on many occasions that football gave him more pleasure than anything else in life *except* his family.

THE MARINO FAMILY

Marino first met Claire Veazey when he was a student at Central Catholic High School. They eventually got married a couple of weeks after Dan played in the Super Bowl in 1985. Marino later said in his autobiography, "When people talk about winning a Super Bowl ring, I understand why. It would be a nice accomplishment. But the most important ring in my life is the one I slipped on Claire's finger at St. Regis Catholic Church in Pittsburgh."

The Marinos have six children, four biological (Dan Jr., Michael, Joey, and Alexandra [Ali]) and two adoptive from China (Niki Lin and Lia). Marino once laughingly commented, "They're not quite enough for a full offense, but sometimes, when everyone's on the move, we sure look like one." On his induction into the Pro Football Hall of Fame, Marino said,

> To Claire and the kids, you guys are my true Hall of Famers. You guys are my whole life, you mean every-thing to me. Win or lose, no matter what the situation, the kids and Claire are always there with smiles, hugs, and kisses. Dano, Michael, Joey, Allie, Niki, Lia. I love you guys. Claire, we've had 21 years together. You've been my best friend. You've been an incredible mom. I can't imagine where I'd be without you.

Just because Marino was a star quarterback, it did not mean he was exempt from the problems of life. Dan and Claire's second son, Michael, was born in 1988. His parents thought that, "He was such a well-behaved baby because he slept great, he didn't really cry, but then we began to realize something wasn't normal about it all. He wouldn't talk, he didn't really have any social dealings with other kids or his brother. He would just sit up in his crib." In 1991, after a series of tests, it turned out that Michael had autism.

Dan and Claire Marino's second son, Michael, was diagnosed with autism—a brain development disorder that impairs social interaction and communication—when he was two years old. Shortly thereafter, the Marinos established the Dan Marino Foundation, which supports medical research, treatment, and outreach programs for children with chronic illnesses and learning or developmental disabilities. Dan and Michael are pictured here at a Miami Heat game in May 2004.

REACHING OUT

Autism is a disorder of the brain that appears early in life, usually before the age of three. Children with autism have problems with social interaction, imagination, play activities, and behavior. The disorder makes it hard for them to communicate with other people and relate to the outside world. More than 400,000 people in the United States have some form of autism. Kids with autism grow up to be adults with autism, but the seriousness of the problems varies greatly from person to person. Michael only has a mild form of autism, and he eventually began attending mainstream schools. At the time of the diagnosis, however, the Marinos were devastated.

Naturally, Claire and Dan became interested in research, treatment, and possible cures for autism. In March 1992, when Michael was four years old, Dan and Claire established the Dan Marino Foundation to support medical research, treatment, and outreach programs for children with chronic illnesses and learning or developmental disabilities. The foundation raises money and distributes it to worthwhile charities, mostly in the South Florida area. It has distributed more than $20 million to more than 30 agencies supporting autism research, services, and treatment programs.

In trying to find the best care for Michael, the Marinos realized there was a need for a complete medical center for children with special needs. In 1995, they created the Dan Marino Center in Weston, Florida, as part of Miami Children's Hospital. The Dan Marino Center provides families a "one-stop shop" for children with special medical needs such as autism, attention deficit disorder (ADD), and brain tumors. The center sees approximately 50,000 children a year for testing, diagnosing, and treating a variety of developmental and psychological disabilities.

Marino said of Michael's care, "We were fortunate we could afford to bring in specialists in the house and we brought people in to help him every day." The family had the resources to hire occupational therapists, physical therapists, and one-on-one teachers. "That's where the idea for the center came about," Marino told CBSsportsline.com. "It's a place where people who may not have the same resources can bring their children to get diagnosed and treated."

In 1998, Dan and Claire Marino opened Child NETT to help children who have special needs resulting from attention deficit disorder, autism, and related disorders. One feature of

WALTER PAYTON NFL MAN OF THE YEAR AWARD

The NFL has had public relations problems in the 2000s. Many players, some quite famous, have been accused or found guilty of criminal actions ranging from drunk driving to murder. However, there is a list of players a football fan can feel confident in supporting. The Walter Payton NFL Man of the Year Award is given annually by the NFL to honor a player's volunteer and charity work, as well as his excellence on the football field. The award has been presented every year since 1970 but was renamed in 1999 for running back Walter Payton, who died that year (Payton won the 1977 award). Each year, every team nominates one player, and a panel of judges selects the winner of the award. The Man of the Year winner receives a $25,000 donation in his name to the charity of his choice, and the other 31 finalists receive $1,000 each. The finalists are all football players who have gone out of their way to build a better world.

WALTER PAYTON NFL MAN OF THE YEAR AWARD WINNERS

Year	Player	Position	Team
2006	Drew Brees/	Quarterback	New Orleans Saints
	LaDainian Tomlinson	Running back	San Diego Chargers
2005	Peyton Manning	Quarterback	Indianapolis Colts
2004	Warrick Dunn	Running back	Atlanta Falcons
2003	Will Shields	Offensive guard	Kansas City Chiefs
2002	Troy Vincent	Cornerback	Philadelphia Eagles
2001	Jerome Bettis	Running back	Pittsburgh Steelers
2000	Derrick Brooks/	Linebacker	Tampa Bay Buccaneers
	Jim Flanigan	Defensive tackle	Chicago Bears
1999	Cris Carter	Wide receiver	Minnesota Vikings
1998	Dan Marino	Quarterback	Miami Dolphins
1997	Troy Aikman	Quarterback	Dallas Cowboys

(continues)

(continued)			
1996	Darrell Green	Cornerback	Washington Redskins
1995	Boomer Esiason	Quarterback	New York Jets
1994	Junior Seau	Linebacker	San Diego Chargers
1993	Derrick Thomas	Linebacker	Kansas City Chiefs
1992	John Elway	Quarterback	Denver Broncos
1991	Anthony Munoz	Offensive tackle	Cincinnati Bengals
1990	Mike Singletary	Linebacker	Chicago Bears
1989	Warren Moon	Quarterback	Houston Oilers
1988	Steve Largent	Wide receiver	Seattle Seahawks
1987	Dave Duerson	Safety	Chicago Bears
1986	Reggie Williams	Linebacker	Cincinnati Bengals
1985	Dwight Stephenson	Center	Miami Dolphins

it is Childnett.tv, a free online television channel dedicated to helping children by providing parents with the latest information in video form on a variety of developmental disorders. Videos can be accessed at *http://www.childnett.tv/videos/services/welcome_childnett_tv*.

Marino has teamed with other celebrities to raise awareness about autism. He said, "I just set out to throw a football. It feels great making a difference." In recognition of his charitable work, Marino won the NFL Man of the Year Award in 1998, the only NFL-sponsored award that recognizes player community service, as well as excellence on the field.

HOLLYWOOD DAN

Beyond fund-raising for his foundation, Marino seemed a little aimless in retirement. His main job was to work as a television

After retiring from football in 2000, Dan Marino has been involved with many endeavors, including acting, but he is best known for his role as an analyst on the *NFL Today*. The show airs each Sunday during the NFL season, and is hosted by James Brown (center). Also pictured here, from left to right, are analysts Shannon Sharpe, Marino, Bill Cowher, and Boomer Esiason.

analyst for a couple of football shows. It kept him in touch with the football life he missed so much. Most people felt he performed his job in a solid but unspectacular way.

Marino seemed to take more pleasure from living bits and pieces of the celebrity lifestyle. After his retirement, he said, "My football career has opened the door to a funhouse of perks like that movie [*Ace Ventura: Pet Detective*]. Things I never dreamed of. Things I never *considered* dreaming of." Marino particularly enjoyed working in movies and videos. He guest-starred as himself in an episode of *The Simpsons*.

Marino also performed cameo roles in several movies. He appeared in a music video by Hootie and the Blowfish, a popular rock group.

Of all his work in movies and television, the best known is definitely the movie *Ace Ventura: Pet Detective*. This silly 1994 comedy starred Jim Carrey, Courtney Cox, Tone Lōc, and Sean Young. Marino portrayed himself as the quarterback of the Dolphins; he had a major role in the story and a good deal of screen time. The story follows the adventures of Ace Ventura (Carrey), a bizarre detective who specializes in cases involving pet animals. Ventura is searching for "Snowflake," the missing mascot of the Miami Dolphins. This film was a surprising box-office hit and eventually grossed more than $70 million in the United States. It helped Carrey establish himself as one of the highest-paid comedians in Hollywood. The movie also was one of the best-selling videos of the 1990s. It indirectly extended Marino's fame far beyond his core football audience.

In 2007, Marino tried a new role. He and his agent, Ralph Springer, along with writer/producer Jerry Davis, combined to produce the movie *Shanghai Hotel*, which publicized the problem of human trafficking and sexual slavery. "It's the passion of Jerry Davis and Ralph that got me involved," Marino said. "It's a story that needed be told and hopefully we did a good job of that." The film tells the story of a young woman who flees China for a new life in the United States, where she is sold into prostitution. Marino invested money in the movie and helped raise additional funds. As always, his mere connection with the film raised its profile and generated media interest.

Marino also tried his hand at business. He opened several restaurant/taverns with mixed results in South Florida and even one in Las Vegas. Marino also did advertisements . . . a lot of advertisements. He tried to convince television viewers to buy, use, or patronize specific restaurants, weight-loss systems, car dealerships, mattresses, pizza chains, banks, jewelry stores, and gloves. He certainly was not doing it for the money.

In 2007, the Marino family lived in a 15,000+-square-foot home in Weston, Florida, with a guesthouse and staff quarters valued at approximately $14 million. The family also had vacation homes in Myrtle Beach (South Carolina), San Francisco (California), and Laramie (Wyoming).

If anything, the commercials seemed like a way for Marino to keep his name in the spotlight. Like many former athletes, he seemed, to a certain degree, to equate anonymity with death. It was hard after performing for so many years in front of millions of fans to watch others fill the same function. Yet it was a role Marino would have to get used to as the years of his retirement began to stretch out before him.

THE POST-MARINO DOLPHINS

Despite his success outside of football, the sport continued to lure Marino. In his role as football analyst, he had the opportunity to see the post-Marino Dolphins close up. It was not a pretty sight. In 2000, Marino's first year in retirement, the story was distressingly familiar. Dolphins coach Dave Wannstedt chose Jay Fiedler as the starting quarterback despite Marino's desire that Damon Huard serve as his successor. The team went 11–5 and won the AFC East Division title for the first time since 1994. In a wild-card playoff game, Miami beat Indianapolis and their young quarterback, Peyton Manning, 23-17, in overtime. It seemed to be a new Miami Dolphins; running back Lamar Smith had an astonishing 40 carries for 209 yards in the victory, including the game-winning 17-yard touchdown in overtime.

However, the wheels came off, as they so often did in the Marino years, in the divisional round of the playoffs. The Oakland Raiders scored 20 points in the first half, recorded 140 rushing yards, and forced four turnovers to shut out the Dolphins, 27-0. In the absence of Dan Marino and Jimmy Johnson, the Dolphins were no better or no worse than the previous 10 years.

The years that followed were no better. The Dolphins went through 10 quarterbacks in seven years trying to replace Marino. They tried rookies and veterans, big-name stars and little-known journeymen. When the Dolphins signed veteran Trent Green to quarterback the team in 2007, he simply noted, "You're not going to find anyone to replace Dan Marino."

The continued mediocrity of the Dolphins bothered Marino. In addition, he missed having a closer connection to the game than just sitting in the television booth as an analyst. He had once ruled out coaching, saying, "There is no way I can coach the guys that play today." However, in January 2004, Marino requested a full-time executive position with the Miami Dolphins. The Dolphins quickly responded by creating the post of senior vice president of football operations. Marino was once again the public face of the Miami Dolphins.

Yet only three weeks later, Marino surprised everyone and resigned. "I knew it would involve a significant lifestyle change," Marino said in his resignation statement. "But after further reflection, it became clear that those adjustments were ones that my family and I are not prepared to make at this time." Instead, Marino returned to the easier life of television commentary. Dolphins owner Wayne Huizenga said, "Needless to say, we're disappointed. Dan is a great guy and we like him a lot. He would have been good for this organization."

However, Don Strock, Marino's mentor and close friend, had the last word. Strock said that Marino was "his own man. I'm sure his family became involved, and they decided what was best for them. He has to do what is right. But I know one day—I don't know when—he's going to be back in football."

In Perspective

In the first years of his retirement, the honors rolled in for Dan Marino. The Miami Dolphins retired Marino's jersey number, 13. It was only the second number retired by the Dolphins to that point (the first was Bob Griese's number 12). The Dolphins also installed a life-size bronze statue of Marino in front of their stadium and changed the name of Stadium Street to Dan Marino Boulevard. In 2002, Marino was inducted into the College Football Hall of Fame in recognition of his outstanding career at the University of Pittsburgh.

HALL OF FAME QUARTERBACK
The culmination of these honors took place in 2005, when Marino was voted into the Pro Football Hall of Fame in the first year of his eligibility. He was the sixth quarterback from

western Pennsylvania to enter the Hall of Fame following Jim Kelly, Joe Montana, Johnny Unitas, George Blanda, and Joe Namath. Hundreds of Dolphins fans traveled to Canton, Ohio, for Marino's induction in August 2005.

Marino made an emotional speech at his induction. He thanked his fellow players and coaches through the years, including his high school and college coaches. He called Don Shula the "greatest coach ever." He specifically thanked the Marks Brothers—Mark Clayton and Mark Duper—center Dwight Stephenson, and quarterback Don Strock. Stephenson noted, "You've got to give Dan a lot of credit, he's the first one to go out and say that he's had great wide receivers, and great coaches. He's the guy who spreads the credit around. I think that's the part that makes Dan so special and most great players special."

After thanking his family, Marino did something unique. Having completed 538 passes to Mark Clayton, Marino wanted to do it one more time. He had originally planned to throw the ball as far as he could, but when he noticed Clayton in the audience, he surprised the ex-Dolphin by instructing him to "go long." Marino licked his fingers as he did for 17 seasons in Miami, took a football from his son, and hit Clayton with a perfect spiral.

Yet as Marino's active career fades further into memory, what will remain? His numerous football accomplishments will certainly be remembered. Marino was selected to play in nine Pro Bowls (1983–1987, 1991–1992, 1994–1995), seven times as a starter. Then there are the 61,361 passing yards in the regular season added to the 4,510 yards in the playoffs. That is a distance greater than the length of the English Channel, five times the size of Mount Everest, or 650 football fields from **goal line** to goal line.

Nor are the accomplishments solely individual. With Marino as quarterback, the Dolphins were perennial playoff contenders. His record as a starting quarterback for Miami was 147–93. The Dolphins reached the postseason in 10 of Marino's 17 seasons. As of 2008, Marino ranked third in NFL

Dan Marino rears back to throw a pass to former teammate Mark Clayton during Marino's induction into the Pro Football Hall of Fame on August 7, 2005. After spotting Clayton in the audience, Marino told his all-time favorite target to "go long" one last time.

history with 37 fourth-quarter comebacks and also third for most victories (147). (John Elway is first in the former category and Brett Favre is second in the latter.)

When he retired, Marino owned 25 NFL records and shared five others. However, it is inevitable that many of these records will be broken as the years go by. In 2004, Pittsburgh Steelers quarterback Ben Roethlisberger broke most of Marino's records for a rookie quarterback. The same year, Peyton Manning eclipsed Marino's touchdown record, throwing 49 touchdowns in a single season, as well as having five consecutive games of four or more touchdown passes. When Marino set those incredible records in 1984, they seemed safe for many years to come, if not for all time. Yet they barely lasted two decades.

Even some of Marino's career records have been surpassed. Green Bay quarterback Bret Favre passed for more than 3,000 yards for the sixteenth consecutive season in 2007. In 2006, he broke Marino's record for career completions. In the fourth game of the 2007 season, Favre broke Marino's record for most touchdown passes in a career in a 23-16 win over the Minnesota Vikings and then broke Marino's record for most career passing yards on December 16 in a 33-14 win over the St. Louis Rams. Lurking in the shadows is Peyton Manning, who is on course to eclipse many of these records if he stays healthy and plays long enough.

As the records fall, Marino may be remembered longer as "the quarterback without the Super Bowl ring." For example, in 2007, *USA Today* opened an article on a spelling bee with this curious comparison:

> **Last chance for spelling bee favorite**
> At this year's Scripps National Spelling Bee, 13-year-old Samir Patel is trying to avoid becoming the Dan Marino of spelling. Samir, a Dallas Cowboys fan from Colleyville, Texas, knows all about Marino's 17-year Hall of Fame career as the Miami Dolphins' quarterback, in which he set records but never won a championship.

This issue of not having won an NFL championship does not seem to dog Hall of Fame quarterbacks Jim Kelly or Fran

Tarkenton in quite the same way. Perhaps it is because they went to the Super Bowl more often than Marino (Kelly—four times; Tarkenton—three times). Maybe it is because the media is fixated on this angle of Marino's career. However, Marino himself has been guilty of returning to the issue again and again. He cannot seem to let go of the passionate competitiveness he learned on the streets of Pittsburgh. In retirement, he seems to feel there is something missing from his career, from his legacy, and it can never be rectified. As often as he tells reporters he would not trade his career for a Super Bowl ring, he never quite seems to believe it himself. So the story continues to linger.

When Marino retired in 2000, a reporter asked him, "How difficult was it to come to this decision without ever having won a Super Bowl?" Marino responded, "That was the burning desire . . . that is what I play for. That was the only reason really to continue to play—did I feel that I was going to have a chance to win a Super Bowl, and that has been a dream of mine my whole career and I am not going to have that chance. But it does not take away from what I have done personally." That same year, Marino made a brief cameo appearance in the Adam Sandler film *Little Nicky*, where he asked Satan for a Super Bowl ring. Five years later, it was still on Marino's mind. He admitted, "I think about it a lot, but not as much as I used to." In another interview, he admitted, "I'd trade every record we broke to be Super Bowl champs." Marino refuses to wear his 1984 AFC Championship ring, calling it "a loser's ring."

Essentially, the valuation of Marino's career comes down to a philosophical issue. Would a person be willing to trade a 17-year record-breaking career in exchange for a Super Bowl ring and five average years? Marino likes to tell the story of his friend Tom Flynn. Flynn was a high school star in western Pennsylvania at the same time as Marino. Flynn went to Pitt and became Marino's college roommate. He played safety on the great Panthers teams and was a fifth-round draft choice

Although Dan Marino never won a Super Bowl during his 17-year career, he is one of the greatest quarterbacks in NFL history. Here, Marino thanks his fans during a ceremony to retire his jersey at halftime of the Dolphins' game with the Baltimore Ravens on September 17, 2000, at Pro Player Stadium in Miami. Marino is joined onstage by his family, from left to right: his son Dan Jr.; wife, Claire; daughter Niki; daughter Alexandria; son Joey; and son Michael (behind Marino).

(number 127 overall) of the Green Bay Packers in 1984. Flynn led the Packers in interceptions as a rookie with nine but only had two more interceptions the rest of his career. The Packers cut him in the middle of the 1986 season. The New York Giants signed Flynn for the last two games of that season. Flynn blocked a punt in the Giants' last regular-season game, made the Super Bowl roster, and won a Super Bowl ring with the Giants. Marino concludes the story, "I'm happy for Tommy. I really am. He's a good friend. But if you're asking whether I'd trade my career for his ring." But then comes the inevitable caveat, as Marino adds, "That's not to say I haven't missed out on something."

Marino's most lasting legacy may be his contributions to the community. He has helped raised millions of dollars for the Dan Marino Center at Miami Children's Hospital. He and his wife created the Dan Marino Foundation to work with children's charities in South Florida. He has raised awareness about autism and participated in numerous charitable fund-raisers. On a personal level, he has often spent time with sick and terminally ill children. Marino himself noted that, "Having a family of my own has taught me about life. . . . Michael [his autistic son] helped me understand more about life and what's important. . . . Our experience with Michael has put things in perspective."

Yet in the end, Marino's ability to make a mark on his community only came about because of his ability to throw a football. Regardless of the records or the ring, that simple pleasure of throwing the football in front of a crowd was always what life was all about for Marino. He said it best in his autobiography:

> Football is what I loved. Football is what drove me. Football always has been my singular passion and constant companion. I've been fortunate enough to travel the world, appear in movies, be in music videos, grace the most popular magazine covers, talk on the biggest talk shows, and get to know some of the world's most famous celebrities. All that is nice. It's wonderful, really. But nothing gave me the rush quite like running out with the team for a big game, in a packed stadium, on a Sunday on a sunny afternoon. Or Saturday on a snowy evening. Or Monday on a nationally televised night. It didn't matter when or where. Throwing a football brought me the most fun and the biggest pleasure of anything outside of my family.

DAN MARINO
POSITION: Quarterback

FULL NAME: Daniel Constantine Marino Jr.
BORN: September 15, 1961, Pittsburgh, Pennsylvania
HEIGHT: 6'4"
WEIGHT: 218 lbs.

COLLEGE: University of Pittsburgh
TEAM: Miami Dolphins (1983–1999)

YEAR	TEAM	G	COMP	ATT	PCT	YD	Y/A	TD	INT
1983	MIA	11	173	296	58.4	2,210	7.5	20	6
1984	MIA	16	362	564	64.2	5,084	9.0	48	17
1985	MIA	16	336	567	59.3	4,137	7.3	30	21
1986	MIA	16	378	623	60.7	4,746	7.6	44	23
1987	MIA	12	263	444	59.2	3,245	7.3	26	13
1988	MIA	16	354	606	58.4	4,434	7.3	28	23
1989	MIA	16	308	550	56.0	3,997	7.3	24	22
1990	MIA	16	306	531	57.6	3,563	6.7	21	11
1991	MIA	16	318	549	57.9	3,970	7.2	25	13
1992	MIA	16	330	554	59.6	4,116	7.4	24	16
1993	MIA	5	91	150	60.7	1,218	8.1	8	3
1994	MIA	16	385	615	62.6	4,453	7.2	30	17
1995	MIA	14	309	482	64.1	3,668	7.6	24	15
1996	MIA	13	221	373	59.2	2,795	7.5	17	9
1997	MIA	16	319	548	58.2	3,780	6.9	16	11
1998	MIA	16	310	537	57.7	3,497	6.5	23	15
1999	MIA	11	204	369	55.3	2,448	6.6	12	17
TOTALS		242	4,967	8,358	59.4	61,361	7.3	420	252

CHRONOLOGY

1961   September 15   Dan Marino is born in Pittsburgh, Pennsylvania.

1976   University of Pittsburgh football team wins its first national title since 1937.

1976–1978   Marino plays quarterback for Central Catholic High School.

1979   June   Kansas City Royals select Marino in the fourth round of the Major League Baseball draft.

1979–1983   Marino attends the University of Pittsburgh.

1979   Pitt goes 11–1 in Marino's freshman season; defeats the University of Arizona, 16-10, in the Fiesta Bowl and finishes sixth in the nation.

1980   Pitt goes 11–1 in Marino's sophomore season; defeats South Carolina, 37-9, in the Gator Bowl and finishes second in the nation.

1981   Pitt goes 11–1 in Marino's junior season for the third consecutive year; defeats Georgia, 24-20, in the Sugar Bowl and again finishes second in the nation; Marino finishes fourth in Heisman Trophy voting.

1982   Marino has a subpar senior season as Pitt goes 9–3; loses to SMU, 7-3, in the Cotton Bowl and finishes ninth in the nation.

1983   January   Marino is selected number one overall in the inaugural USFL draft but does not sign.
April   Picked twenty-seventh by the Miami Dolphins in the NFL draft—he is the sixth quarterback taken.
September 19   Makes his NFL debut and throws his first completion (nine-yard pass to Mark Duper), followed by first touchdown pass (six yards to Joe Rose).
October 9   Starts his first NFL game and completes 14 of 20 passes for 268 yards and three touchdowns.

Leads Dolphins to AFC East Division title with 12–4 record and wins Rookie of the Year by throwing for 2,210 yards, with 20 touchdown passes and only six interceptions.

1984   Marino has best season of his career and one of the best of all time; sets passing records for touchdowns (48), passing yards (5,084), and completions (362); first quarterback to throw for more than 5,000 yards in a season; also sets the record for number of games passing for 300 yards or more (nine) and number of games passing for 400 yards or more (four).

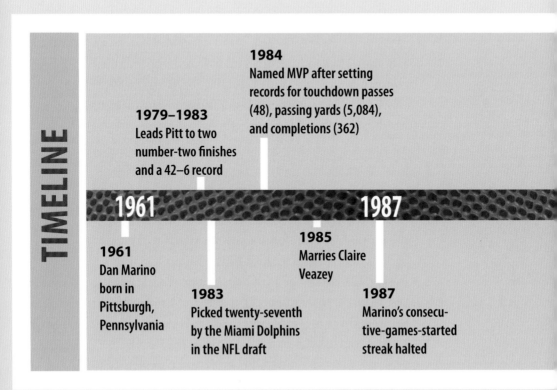

TIMELINE

1979–1983
Leads Pitt to two number-two finishes and a 42–6 record

1984
Named MVP after setting records for touchdown passes (48), passing yards (5,084), and completions (362)

1961

1987

1961
Dan Marino born in Pittsburgh, Pennsylvania

1983
Picked twenty-seventh by the Miami Dolphins in the NFL draft

1985
Marries Claire Veazey

1987
Marino's consecutive-games-started streak halted

1985   Dolphins defeat Seattle Seahawks, 31-10, in divisional
round of playoffs; throws for 421 yards and wins his
only AFC Championship Game as Dolphins defeat
Pittsburgh Steelers, 45-28.

January 20 San Francisco defeats Miami in Super Bowl
XIX, 38-16, in Marino's first and only trip to the big game;
February Marries Claire Veazey; they will have six
children together: four biological and two adopted.

Marino and Miami score 31 points in the first half and
defeat the previously unbeaten Chicago Bears,
38-24, in one of most-watched regular-season games

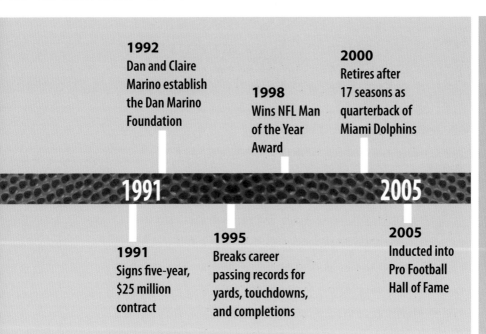

1992
Dan and Claire
Marino establish
the Dan Marino
Foundation

1998
Wins NFL Man
of the Year
Award

2000
Retires after
17 seasons as
quarterback of
Miami Dolphins

1991

2005

1991
Signs five-year,
$25 million
contract

1995
Breaks career
passing records for
yards, touchdowns,
and completions

2005
Inducted into
Pro Football
Hall of Fame

DAN MARINO

in NFL history; Miami goes 12–4 and wins AFC East Division title.

1986   New England Patriots stun Dolphins in AFC Championship Game, 31-14.
Marino's second-best season; throws for NFL-leading 4,746 yards and 44 touchdowns.
September 21 Marino and Ken O'Brien of the New York Jets combine to set NFL single-game records of 884 passing yards and 10 touchdown passes (Marino completes 30 of 50 passes for 448 yards and six touchdowns in the game).
November 24 Marino completes 29 of 36 passes as 5–6 Dolphins stun 10–1 Jets, 45-3.

1987   Marino's consecutive-game streak as starting quarterback broken by NFL players strike; leads AFC in touchdown passes and completions.

1988   Marino becomes first NFL quarterback to pass for more than 4,000 yards four times in a career.
October 23 Jets defeat Dolphins, 44-30, as Marino passes for 521 yards—fourth highest of all time—but also throws five interceptions.

1990–1991   Dolphins go 12–4 in 1990; defeat Kansas City Chiefs, 17-16, in first round of the playoffs behind Marino's spectacular fourth-quarter performance.
Marino signs a five-year, $25 million contract (the largest contract in NFL history to that date).

1992   Danand Claire Marino establish the Dan Marino Foundation; Miami goes 11–5 and wins AFC East Division.

1993   Marinoleads Dolphins to first-round playoff victory over San Diego Chargers, 31-0; Buffalo defeats Miami, 29-10, in Marino's last appearance in an AFC Championship Game.
Marino tears Achilles tendon; misses most of 1993 season.

1994   Marino has major role in the movie *Ace Ventura: Pet Detective.*

September 4 In first regular-season game after injury, Marino completes 23 of 42 passes for 473 yards and five touchdowns as Dolphins beat the Patriots, 39-35; November 27 Dolphins defeat Jets, 28-24, in the "Clock Play" game.

Dolphins win AFC East Division title with 10–6 record; Marino receives Comeback Player of the Year Award.

1995   Dan and Claire Marino establish the Dan Marino Center in Weston, Florida, as part of Miami Children's Hospital; Marino breaks career passing records formerly held by Fran Tarkenton for yards, touchdowns, and completions; in playoff loss to Buffalo, Marino throws record-tying 64 passes, completing 33 for 422 yards; Don Shula retires as Dolphins coach, replaced by Jimmy Johnson.

1996   Marino throws 4,000th completion and exceeds 50,000 yards in total passing yardage for his career.

1998   Dan and Claire Marino create Child NETT; Marino wins NFL Man of the Year Award.

1999   December 27 In Marino's last game against the Jets, he passes for 322 yards and three touchdowns in a 38-31 loss.

2000   Marino rallies team in wild-card playoff game against Seattle Seahawks—throws for 196 yards and a touchdown, leading Dolphins to first playoff road win of his career.

March 13 Marino retires after 17 seasons as quarterback of Miami Dolphins.

2001   Miami Dolphins retire Marino's number 13 jersey.

2002   Marino inducted into the College Football Hall of Fame.

2005   Marino inducted into the Pro Football Hall of Fame.

GLOSSARY

American Football Conference (AFC)   One of the two conferences in the National Football League (NFL). The AFC was established after the NFL merged with the American Football League (AFL) in 1970.

audible   A play called by the quarterback at the line of scrimmage to change the play called in the huddle.

backup   A second-string player who does not start the game, but comes in later in relief of a starter.

blitz   A defensive maneuver in which one or more linebackers or defensive backs, who normally remain behind the line of scrimmage, instead charge into the opponent's backfield.

blocking   When a player obstructs another player's path with his body. Examples: cut block, zone block, trap block, pull block, screen block, pass block, and double-team block.

bootleg   An offensive play predicated upon misdirection in which the quarterback pretends to hand the ball to another player and then carries the ball in the opposite direction of the supposed ballcarrier with the intent of either passing or running (sometimes the quarterback has the option of doing either).

center   A player position on offense. The center snaps the ball.

chain   The 10-yard-long chain that is used by the chain crew (aka, "chain gang") to measure for a new series of downs.

completion percentage   The percentage of passes thrown by a player that are completed. For example, if a running back throws one pass all season and completes it, his completion percentage would be 100 percent.

cornerback   A defensive back who lines up near the line of scrimmage across from a wide receiver. His primary job is to disrupt passing routes and to defend against short and medium passes in the passing game and to contain the rusher on running plays.

defensive back   A cornerback or safety position on the defensive team; commonly defends against wide receivers on passing plays. Generally there are four defensive backs playing at a time.

defensive end   A player position on defense who lines up on the outside of the defensive line whose principal function is to deliver pressure to the quarterback.

defensive tackle   A player position on defense on the inside of the defensive line whose principal function is to contain the run.

drive   A continuous set of offensive plays gaining substantial yardage and several first downs, usually leading to a scoring opportunity.

end zone   The area between the end line and the goal line, bounded by the sidelines.

extra point   A single point scored in a conversion attempt by making what would be a field goal by place- or drop-kicking the ball through the opponent's goal.

field goal   Score of three points made by place- or drop-kicking the ball through the opponent's goal.

first down   The first of a set of four downs. Usually, a team that has a first down needs to advance the ball 10 yards to receive another first down, but penalties or field position (i.e., less than 10 yards from the opposing end zone) can affect this.

formation   An arrangement of the offensive skill players.

fourth down   The final of a set of four downs. Unless a first down is achieved or a penalty forces a replay of the down, the team will lose control of the ball after this play. If a team does not think they can get a first down, they often punt on fourth down or kick a field goal if they are close enough to do so.

fullback   A player position on offense. In modern formations, this position may be varied, and this player has more blocking responsibilities in comparison to the halfback or tailback.

fumble   A ball that a player accidentally loses possession of.

goal line   The front of the end zone.

guard   One of two player positions on offense (linemen).

handoff   A player's handing of a live ball to another player. The handoff goes either backwards or laterally, as opposed to a forward pass.

holding   There are two kinds of holding: offensive holding, illegally blocking a player from the opposing team by grabbing and holding his uniform or body; and defensive holding, called against defensive players who impede receivers who are more than five yards from the line of scrimmage, but who are not actively making an attempt to catch the ball.

huddle   An on-field gathering of members of a team in order to secretly communicate instructions for the upcoming play.

incomplete pass   A forward pass of the ball that no player legally caught.

interception   The legal catching of a forward pass thrown by an opposing player.

kickoff   A free kick that starts each half, or restarts the game following a touchdown or field goal.

line of scrimmage/scrimmage line   One of two vertical planes parallel to the goal line when the ball is to be put in play by scrimmage.

linebacker   A player position on defense. The linebackers typically play one to six yards behind the defensive linemen and are the most versatile players on the field because they can play both run and pass defense or are called to blitz.

man-to-man coverage   A defense in which all players in pass coverage, typically linebackers and defensive backs, cover a specific player.

National Collegiate Athletic Association (NCAA)   Principal governing body of college sports, including college football.

National Football Conference (NFC)   One of the two conferences in the National Football League (NFL). The NFC was established after the NFL merged with the American Football League (AFL) in 1970.

National Football League (NFL)   The largest professional American football league, with 32 teams.

offside   An infraction of the rule that requires both teams to be on their own side of their restraining line as or before the ball is put in play. Offside is normally called on the defensive team.

option   A type of play in which the quarterback has the option of handing off, keeping, or laterally passing to one or more backs. Often described by a type of formation or play action, such as triple option, veer option, or counter option.

pass interference   When a player illegally hinders an eligible receiver's opportunity to catch a forward pass.

passer rating   (*also* **quarterback rating**) A numeric value used to measure the performance of quarterbacks. It was formulated in 1973 and it uses the player's completion percentage, passing yards, touchdowns, and interceptions.

play action   A tactic in which the quarterback fakes either a handoff or a throw in order to draw the defense away from the intended offensive method.

pocket   An area on the offensive side of the line of scrimmage, where the offensive linemen attempt to prevent the defensive players from reaching the quarterback during passing plays.

position   A place where a player plays relative to teammates, and/or a role filled by that player.

punt   A kick in which the ball is dropped and kicked before it reaches the ground. Used to give up the ball to the opposition after offensive downs have been used.

quarterback   An offensive player who lines up behind the center, from whom he takes the snap.

reception   When a player catches (receives) the ball.

running back   A player position on offense. Although the term usually refers to the halfback or tailback, fullbacks are also considered running backs.

sack   Tackling a ballcarrier who intends to throw a forward pass. A sack also is awarded if a player forces a fumble of the ball, or the ballcarrier to go out of bounds, behind the line of scrimmage on an apparent intended forward pass play.

safety   A player position on defense; a method of scoring (worth two points) by downing an opposing ballcarrier in his own end zone, forcing the opposing ballcarrier out of his own end zone and out of bounds, or forcing the offensive team to fumble the ball so that it exits the end zone.

salary cap   A limit on the amount any NFL team can spend on its players' salaries; the salary cap was introduced in 1994 in order to bring parity to the NFL.

scramble   On a called passing play, when the quarterback runs from the pocket in an attempt to avoid being sacked, giving the receivers more time to get open or attempting to gain positive yards by running himself.

secondary   Refers to the defensive "backfield," specifically the safeties and cornerbacks.

shotgun formation   Formation in which offensive team may line up at the start of a play. In this formation, the quarterback receives the snap five to eight yards behind the center.

sideline   One of the lines marking each side of the field.

snap   The handoff or pass from the center that begins a play from scrimmage.

special teams   The units that handle kickoffs, punts, free kicks, and field-goal attempts.

starter   A player who is the first to play his position within a given game or season. Depending on the position and the game situation, this player may be replaced or share time with one or more players later in the game. For example, a quarterback may start the game but be replaced by a backup quarterback if the game becomes one-sided.

tackle   The act of forcing a ballcarrier to the ground.

tailback   Player position on offense farthest ("deepest") back, except in kicking formations.

tight end   A player position on offense, often known as a Y receiver, when he lines up on the line of scrimmage, next to the offensive tackle. Tight ends are used as blockers during running plays and either run a route or stay in to block during passing plays.

time of possession   The amount of time one team has the ball in its possession relative to the other team.

touchdown   A play worth six points, accomplished by gaining legal possession of the ball in the opponent's end zone. It also allows the team a chance for one extra point by kicking the ball or a chance to attempt a two-point conversion.

turnover   The loss of the ball by one team to the other team. This is usually the result of a fumble or an interception.

West Coast offense   An offensive philosophy that uses short, high-percentage passes as the core of a ball-control offense.

wide receiver   A player position on offense. He is split wide (usually about 10 yards) from the formation and plays on the line of scrimmage as a split end (X) or one yard off as a flanker (Z).

wild card   The two playoff spots given to the two nondivision-winning teams that have the best records in each conference.

wishbone   A formation involving three running backs lined up behind the quarterback in the shape of a Y, similar to the shape of a wishbone.

yard   One yard of linear distance in the direction of one of the two goals. A field is 100 yards. Typically, a team is required to advance at least 10 yards in order to get a new set of downs.

zone defense   A defense in which players who are in pass coverage cover zones of the field, instead of individual players.

BIBLIOGRAPHY

BOOKS

Brenner, Richard. *Football Superstars Album*. New York: Beech Tree, 1998.

Kennedy, Nick. *Dan Marino: Star Quarterback*. Springfield, N.J.: Enslow Publishers, 1998.

Marino, Dan, and David Hyde. *Dan Marino: My Life in Football*. Chicago: Triumph Books, 2005.

Rambeck, Richard. *Dan Marino*. Plymouth, Minn.: Child's World, 1997.

Sullivan, George. *Quarterbacks!: Eighteen of Football's Greatest*. New York: Atheneum Books for Young Readers, 1998.

WEB SITES

Dan the Man
http://aol.nba.com/heat/news/dan_the_man_051107.html

A Time for Change: Bobby Grier and the 1956 Sugar Bowl
http://www.blackathlete.net/artman/publish/article_01392.shtml

This Marino Miracle Is a Victory over Autism
http://cbs.sportsline.com/nfl/story/5957706

College Football Reference
http://cfreference.net/cfr

Childnett.tv
http://www.childnett.tv/

Dan Marino Page
http://www.dolphinsinfo.com/marinop.htm

Marino Retires after 17 Seasons
http://espn.go.com/nfl/news/2000/0309/412737.html

Making a Run for It—Miami Dolphins' Coach Jimmy Johnson Focuses on 2000 Super Bowl

http://findarticles.com/p/articles/mi_m1208/is_27_223/ai_55198797/pg_2

Dwight Stephenson: Pro Football Hall of Fame Class of 1998

http://www.footballresearch.com/articles/frpage.cfm?topic=4-stephenson

Marino Raises Awareness of Autism

http://www.forbes.com/business/2005/12/07/autism-research-marino-cx_tm_1208danmarino.html

Dan Marino Retirement Press Conference

http://members.aol.com/metzgerdj/transcri.htm

Miami Dolphins Team Page

http://www.nfl.com/teams/miamidolphins/profile?team=MIA

The Pittsburgh Kid

http://www.palmbeachpost.com/dolphins/content/sports/epa-per/2005/07/31/a1b_marino_0731.html

Tony Nathan

http://www.phinatics.com/tonynathan.htm

Cefalo on Dolphins, Past and Present

http://phins.com/chris/column_102305.html

1980 Panthers Rank among Best

http://www.pittsburghpostgazette.net/sports/columnists/20001102smizik.asp

Dan Marino: A Football Player's Journey to Canton

http://www.post-gazette.com/pg/05217/548990.stm

Tradition of Western Pennsylvania Quarterbacks Continues

http://www.post-gazette.com/pg/05238/558775.stm

Dan Marino's Enshrinement Speech Transcript: Pro Football Hall of Fame

http://www.profootballhof.com/enshrinement/release.jsp?release_id=1605

Hall of Famer: Q & A with Dwight Stephenson

http://www.profootballhof.com/history/release.jsp?release_id=435

Hall Recall: Dan Marino

http://www.profootballhof.com/hof/release.jsp?release_id=1585

Uneasy Rests the Alliance of Johnson, Marino

http://www.sportingnews.com/archives/marino/marino-jj.html

Marino's Golden Arm Changed the Game

http://sports.espn.go.com/espn/classic/bio/news/story?page=Marino_Dan

Marino Goes Deep with Emotions

http://www.usatoday.com/sports/columnist/saraceno/2005-08-07-saraceno-marino_x.htm

Green Hopes He's the Answer for Dolphins

http://www.usatoday.com/sports/football/2007-06-07-2814544825_x.htm

FURTHER READING

BOOKS

Dan Marino (A Look Back at a Legend). Miami: Curtis Publishing, 2000.

Dan Marino: The Making of a Legend. Dallas: Beckett Publications, 1999.

Fiedler, Tom. *Marino: Stories from a Hall of Fame Career*. Chicago: Triumph Books, 2005.

Libero, Rich. *This Could Be the Year: My 30 Years as a Miami Dolphins Fan*. Cranston, R.I.: Writers Collective, 2005.

Marino, Dan. *First & Goal (Positively for Kids)*. Dallas: Taylor Publishing, 1997.

Marvez, Alex. *Stadium Stories: Miami Dolphins: Colorful Tales of the Aqua and Orange*. Guilford, Conn.: Globe Pequot, 2003.

Maxymuk, John. *Strong Arm Tactics: A History and Statistical Analysis of the Professional Quarterback*. Jefferson, N.C.: McFarland, 2007.

McDonough, Will. *The NFL Century: The Complete Story of the National Football League, 1920–2000*. New York: Smithmark, 1999.

Schmalzbauer, Adam. *The History of the Miami Dolphins*. Mankato, Minn.: Creative Education, 2004.

Sporting News. Pro Football's Greatest Quarterbacks: the Fab 50: A Ranking of the NFL Legends with Golden Wings. New York: Sporting News, 2004.

Yost, Mark. *Tailgating, Sacks, and Salary Caps: How the NFL Became the Most Successful Sports League in History*. Chicago: Kaplan, 2006.

WEB SITES

Dan Marino: The Official Website
http://www.danmarino.com/

Dan Marino Foundation
http://www.danmarinofoundation.org/

Miami Dolphins Official Web site
http://www.miamidolphins.com/newsite/flash_content.asp

National Football League Official Site
http://www.nfl.com/

Pro Football Hall of Fame
http://www.profootballhof.com/

PICTURE CREDITS

INDEX

A

Abdul-Jabbar, Karim, 94
Ace Ventura: Pet Detective, 109–110
Achilles tendon injury, 85–87
adoption, 104
Atlanta Falcons, 67
advertisements, 47–48, 110–111
autism, 104–108, 119

B

Baltimore Colts, 15, 22, 49
Barkley, Charles, 12
Barnett, Bill, 49
baseball, 19, 23–24
Batch, Charlie, 22
Baumhower, Bob, 49
Betters, Doug, 49
birthday of Dan Marino, 16
Blackledge, Todd, 36, 44
Blackwood, Glenn and Lyle, 49
Blanda, George, 8, 22, 114
Bledsoe, Drew, 87
Bokamper, Kim, 49
Bowden, Bobby, 33
Boyarsky, Jerry, 33
Bradshaw, Terry, 22, 91
Brown, James, 109
Brown, John, 36, 38
Brudzinski, Bob, 49
Buffalo Bills, 15, 52, 54, 68, 78,
    81–82, 84–85, 91–92, 96
Bulger, Marc, 22
Buoniconti, Nick, 48
business interests, 110–111

C

Carnegie, Andrew, 17
Carnegie Institute of Technology,
    21, 26
Carrey, Jim, 110
Cascadden, Chad, 71
Cathedral of Learning, 17, 26
Cavanaugh, Matt, 29
Cefalo, Jimmy, 61, 63, 76
Central Catholic High School,
    20–21, 22

champions, defining, 14
Chicago Bears, 67–68, 100
Child NETT, 106–108
Christie, Steve, 85
Cincinnati Bengals, 8, 54
civil rights, 30–31
Clayton, Mark, 52, 59–60, 63, 71,
    81, 114–115
Cleveland Browns, 67, 85
Clock Play, 71, 88–89
clutch players, 8–9
Cobb, Ty, 12
College Football Hall of Fame, 113
Collins, Dwight, 34
Comeback Player of the Year
    Award, 88
confidence, 51, 61–62
Cotton Bowl, 38–39, 40
Covert, Jimbo, 34, 44
Cowher, Bill, 109
Csonka, Larry, 48, 55–56

D

Dallas Cowboys, 62, 67, 77, 93, 94,
    98, 116
Dan Marino Center, 106, 119
Dan Marino Foundation, 105–106,
    119
Davis, Jerry, 110
Dawkins, Julius, 34, 38
defense, rule changes and, 57–59
defensive backs, Super Bowl XIX
    and, 9–10, 11
Denver Broncos, 13, 96
Detroit Lions, 87, 95
Dickerson, Eric, 38
Ditka, Mike, 28
Dolphins. *See* Miami Dolphins
Dorsett, Tony, 25, 28–30, 77
drafts
    Kansas City Royals and, 24
    NFL and, 44–47
    University of Pittsburgh and,
        33–34
    USFL and, 43–44
Duhe, A. J., 70

Dungy, Tony, 63–64
Duper, Mark, 52, 59–61, 63, 70–72, 78, 114

E
Eason, Tony, 44, 68
Edmunds, Ferrell, 84
education, 20
Elway, John, 13–14, 96, 115
endorsements, 47–48, 110–111
Erdelyi, Rich, 21
Erving, Julius, 58
Esiason, Boomer, 79, 109
Evans, Norm, 64

F
Fada, Rob, 34
Favre, Brett, 78, 115, 116
Fazio, Serafino "Foge," 26, 38, 39–40
Fiedler, Jay, 102, 111
Fiesta Bowl, 32, 33
500-yard games, 80–81
Florida State, 32–33
Flutie, Doug, 76
Flynn, Tom, 34, 117–119
Forbes Field, 17
46 Defense, 67
Foster, Roy, 64
Fouts, Dan, 15
free agency, 75, 76–77, 83, 102
Frerotte, Gus, 22
Fryar, Irving, 88, 89
fumbles, Super Bowl XIX and, 11
Fusina, Chuck, 22

G
Gator Bowl, 34, 40
Geisler, Jon, 64
Georgia Tech, 30–31
Gibbs, Joe, 80
Gradkowski, Bruce, 22
Green, Cleveland, 64
Green, Hugh, 32, 33
Green, Trent, 112
Green Bay Packers, 14, 78, 116, 118
Gretzky, Wayne, 58
Grier, Bobby, 30–31

Griese, Bob, 48, 49, 80, 113
Griffin, Marvin, 30–31
Grimm, Russ, 34

H
Hall of Fame, 47, 104, 113–115
Heisman Trophy
    fourth place in 1981 voting for, 37
    George Rogers and, 32, 34
    Herschel Walker and, 40, 42
    ninth place in 1982 voting for, 42, 43
    Tony Dorsett and, 25, 29
Helicopter Catch, 70
Hicks, Dwight, 9
Higgs, Mark, 84
Hollywood, 108–110, 117
Hootie and the Blowfish video, 110
Houston Oilers, 8, 15
Huard, Damon, 98, 100, 111
Huizenga, Wayne, 90–91, 112
human trafficking, 110
Humphries, Stan, 84

I
Indianapolis Colts, 54, 94, 95, 111
Ingram, Mark, 88
injuries
    in 1993 season, 85–87
    in 1999 season, 98
    ankle fracture, 94
    at University of Pittsburgh, 32
interceptions
    first collegiate pass as, 32
    Penn State game and, 35
    senior season and, 37, 38
    Super Bowl XIX and, 11

J
Jackson, Keith, 84, 89
Jackson, Rickey, 33
Jacksonville Jaguars, 100
James, Craig, 38, 77
Jaworski, Ron, 86
Jensen, Jim, 54, 61
Johnson, Dan, 10
Johnson, Jimmy, 93–102

Jones & Laughlin steel mill, 18
Jordan, Michael, 58
Jurgensen, Sonny, 15

K

Kansas City Chiefs, 81, 89
Kansas City Royals, 24
Kelly, Jim, 15, 22, 44, 76, 114, 116–117
Kiick, Jim, 55
Killer B's, 49
Kosar, Bernie, 87
Kuechenberg, Bob, 49, 53, 64

L

Langer, Jim, 48, 64
layoffs, steel industry and, 27
Lee, Ronnie, 64
Lewis, Tim, 44
Little, Larry, 48, 64
Little Nicky, 117
Lombardi, Vince, 14
Long, Howie, 77
Los Angeles Express, 43
Los Angeles Raiders, 52, 77
Lott, Ronnie, 9–10
Lujack, Johnny, 22
Lyons, Marty, 65, 71

M

Majors, Johnny, 28–29
Malone, Karl, 12
Man of the Year Award, 107–108
Manley, Dexter, 78
Manning, Peyton, 111, 116
Marino, Alexandra (daughter), 104
Marino, Cindi (sister), 16
Marino, Claire (wife), 102, 104
Marino, Daniel Jr. (son), 104
Marino, Daniel Sr. (father), 16, 19, 31
Marino, Debbie (sister), 16
Marino, Joey (son), 104
Marino, Lia (daughter), 104
Marino, Michael (son), 104–108, 119
Marino, Niki Lin (daughter), 104
Marino, Veronica (mother), 16
Marino Center, 106, 119

Marino Foundation, 105–106, 119
Marks Brothers, 59–61, 114
Matter of Style, A (Namath), 22
May, Mark, 34
McDuffie, O. J., 61
McIlhenny, Lance, 39
McMillan, Erik, 81
McMillan, Randy, 34
Meisner, Greg, 33
Miami Dolphins
    1985 Chicago Bears game and, 67–68
    after departure of Marino, 111–112
    drafting by, 45–47
        executive position with, 112
    history of, 48–49
    lucrative 1991 contact with, 82
    New York Jets rivalry and, 68–72
    offensive linemen of, 64–65
    overall record with, 114–115
    rookie season at, 52–54
    second season at, 59–66
    Super Bowl XIX and, 7–12
    Minnesota Vikings, 15, 57, 91, 102, 116
Mitchell, Scott, 86–87
Mitchell, Wade, 31
Monday Night Miracle, 71
Monongahela River, 17, 18, 27
monopolies, 78
Montana, Joe
    1982 strike and, 77
    Kansas City and, 89
    Pennsylvania and, 22, 114
    Super Bowl XIX and, 7, 8, 11
Moon, Warren, 15
Moore, Nat, 49, 52, 61, 67, 70
Moore, Wayne, 64
Morris, Eugene "Mercury," 55–56
movies, 109–110, 117
Mud Bowl, 69, 70

N

Namath, Joe, 22, 23, 114
Nathan, Tony, 10, 49, 51, 56, 61, 63
NCAA championship, 22

Neill, Bill, 33
New England Patriots, 63, 68, 78, 87–88, 94, 95–96
New York Giants, 8, 77, 94, 118
New York Jets, 45, 52, 53, 62, 68–72, 80–81, 83–84, 88–89, 98
Newman, Ed, 49, 64
NFL Player of the Year Award, 63
NFL Rookie of the Year Award, 54
NFL Today, 109
Nicola, Frank, 17
Notre Dame, 28–29, 38
number 13, 24, 113, 118

O

Oakland neighborhood (Pittsburgh, Pennsylvania), 16–19
Oakland Raiders, 111
O'Brien, Ken, 45, 69–72
offensive linemen, 64–65

P

Parcells, Bill, 88
Patel, Samir, 116
Paterno, Joe, 39
Payton, Walter, 107–108
Penn State, 35–36, 38, 39–40
Philadelphia Eagles, 15, 84
Pittsburgh, University of
   civil rights and, 30–31
   football history of, 28–31
   playing for, 32–37
   recruitment by, 26
   rooting for as child, 21
   senior season at, 37–41
   statistics at, 40–41
Pittsburgh Steelers, 8, 21, 22, 54, 57, 63, 100, 102, 116
playoffs, summary of, 99
Pony Express, 38
Pro Bowl, 54, 114
Pro Football Hall of Fame, 47, 104, 113–115

Q

quarterbacks, 12–13, 58–59

R

receivers, career completions to, 61
recruitment, 25–27
retirement, 101, 102, 117
revenue sharing, 74–76
Rice, Grantland, 14
Rivera, Gabriel, 44
Robbie, Joe, 90
Robinson, Jimmy Joe, 30
Roethlisberger, Ben, 116
Rogers, Doug, 63
Rogers, George, 32, 34
Rooney, Art, 44
Rosborough, Bob, 31
Rose, Joe, 52, 53
Rozier, Mike, 76

S

sacks, 11, 62–63, 65
St. Louis Cardinals, 62
St. Louis Rams, 68, 116
St. Regis School, 20
salary caps, 83
Sams, Ron, 34
San Diego Chargers, 15, 82, 84, 89
San Francisco 49ers, 7–12, 15, 64, 77
Sandler, Adam, 117
satellite dish, 47
scabs, 74
Schamann, Uwe von, 10
Schenley Park, 17
scholarships, 24
Schubert, Mark, 32
Seattle Seahawks, 8, 54, 63, 98, 100
Sehorn, Jason, 94
Shanghai Hotel, 110
Sharpe, Shannon, 109
Sherrill, Jackie, 29–31, 34–35, 38
Shula, Don
   drafting by, 45–47
   football rule changes and, 57–59
   Miami Dolphins and, 48
   passing game and, 55–56
   resignation of, 90–93
   Super Bowl XIX and, 11
Simpsons, The, 109

Sipe, Brian, 77
Smith, Lamar, 111
Southern Methodist University
    (SMU), 38–39
spelling bee, 116
Springer, Ralph, 110
Staubach, Roger, 59
Steel Curtain, 57
steel industry, 18, 27
Stephenson, Dwight, 49, 64–65, 71,
    114
Stoyanovich, Pete, 89
strikes, 74–78, 83
Strock, Don, 49, 51–52, 112, 114
Sugar Bowl, 29, 30–31, 35–36, 40
summer school, 20
Super Bowl XIX, 7–12
Super Bowl XVI, 8

T

Tarkenton, Fran, 15, 91, 92, 116–117
Taylor, Lawrence, 77
television deals, NFL and, 74, 77
13 (jersey number), 24, 113, 118
Thomas, Lynn, 34
Thompson, David, 58
Thrower, Willie, 22
Tittle, Y. A., 8, 15
Toews, Jeff, 64
Trocano, Rick, 32, 34
Trout, Dave, 34

U

Unitas, Johnny, 22, 114
United States Football League
    (USFL), 43–44, 76–77
University of Arizona, 32, 35
University of Georgia, 29, 34, 35–36,
    39–40
University of Miami, 93, 97
University of Pittsburgh
    civil rights and, 30–31
    football history of, 28–31

playing for, 32–37
recruitment by, 26
rooting for as child, 21
senior season at, 37–41
statistics at, 40–41
University of South Carolina, 32,
    34
USFL (United States Football
    League), 43–44, 76–77

V

Veazey, Claire (wife). See Marino,
    Claire

W

Walker, Herschel, 34, 35–36, 40, 42,
    76
Walter Payton Man of the Year
    Award, 107–108
Wannstedt, Dave, 97, 100, 111
Warfield, Paul, 48
Warhol, Andy, 18, 26
Warner, Kurt, 68
Washington Redskins, 15, 49, 50, 62,
    78, 80, 100
Webb, Richmond, 65
White, Danny, 77
White, Reggie, 76
Williams, Mike, 89
Williams, Ted, 12
Williamson, Carlton, 9, 34
Wilson, August, 20–21
Woodley, David, 49, 50, 51, 52
Woodstrock, 49
Wright, Eric, 9

Y

Young, Steve, 76

ABOUT THE AUTHOR

JON STERNGASS is the author of *First Resorts: Pursuing Pleasure at Saratoga Springs, Newport, and Coney Island*. He currently is a freelance writer specializing in children's nonfiction books; his most recent work for Chelsea House is a history of Filipino-Americans and a biography of José Martí. Born and raised in Brooklyn, New York, Sterngass has a B.A. in history and philosophy from Franklin and Marshall College, an M.A. from the University of Wisconsin-Milwaukee in medieval history, and a Ph.D. from City University of New York in American history. He has resided in Saratoga Springs, New York, for 15 years with his wife, Karen Weltman, and sons, Eli (13) and Aaron (10). One of his fondest memories as a football fan is Dan Marino's last-second touchdown pass to John Brown that helped Pittsburgh defeat Georgia in the 1982 Sugar Bowl.